knit one,
Embellish Too

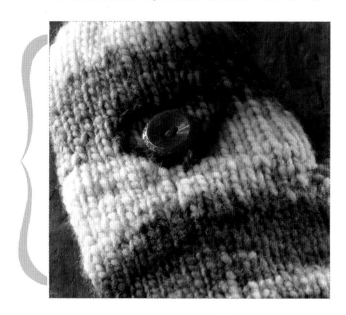

*Hats, Mittens and Scarves
with a Twist*

BY COSETTE CORNELIUS-BATES

NORTH LIGHT BOOKS
CINCINNATI, OHIO

www.mycraftivity.com

12 11 10 09 08   5 4 3 2 1

Library of Congress Cataloging-in-Publication Data

Cornelius-Bates, Cosette
  Knit one, embellish too : hats, mittens, and scarves with a twist / by Cosette Cornelius-Bates. -- 1st ed.
     p. cm.
  Includes index.
  ISBN 978-1-60061-046-2
  1. Knitting--Patterns. 2. Hats. 3. Mittens. 4. Scarves.
I. Title.
  TT825.C687 2008
  746.43'2041--dc22
                    2007043135

Distributed in Canada by Fraser Direct
100 Armstrong Avenue
Georgetown, ON, Canada L7G 5S4
Tel: (905) 877-4411

Distributed in the U.K. and Europe by David & Charles
Brunel House, Newton Abbot, Devon, TQ12 4PU, England
Tel: (+44) 1626 323200, Fax: (+44) 1626 323319
E-mail: postmaster@davidandcharles.co.uk

Distributed in Australia by Capricorn Link
P.O. Box 704, South Windsor, NSW 2756 Australia
Tel: (02) 4577-3555

Metric Conversion Chart

TO CONVERT	TO	MULTIPLY BY
Inches	Centimeters	2.54
Centimeters	Inches	0.4
Feet	Centimeters	30.5
Centimeters	Feet	0.03
Yards	Meters	0.9
Meters	Yards	1.1
Sq. Inches	Sq. Centimeters	6.45
Sq. Centimeters	Sq. Inches	0.16
Sq. Feet	Sq. Meters	0.09
Sq. Meters	Sq. Feet	10.8
Sq. Yards	Sq. Meters	0.8
Sq. Meters	Sq. Yards	1.2
Pounds	Kilograms	0.45
Kilograms	Pounds	2.2
Ounces	Grams	28.3
Grams	Ounces	0.035

fw
F+W PUBLICATIONS, INC.
www.fwpublications.com

Editor: Jennifer Claydon
Designer: Marissa Bowers
Layout Artist: Cheryl Mathauer
Production Coordinator: Greg Nock
Technical Illustrators: Toni Toomey, Kara Gott
and Cheryl Mathauer
Photographers: Adam Leigh-Manuell,
John Carrico, and Adam Henry of Alias Imaging, LLC
Stylists: Jan Nickum and Leslie Brinkley
Make-up Artist: Cass Smith

Dedication

For my parents, Marian and Dana,
who have supported me even when they weren't quite sure what I was doing.

Acknowledgments

Alissa, I wouldn't have done this book without your encouragement, so thank you. To Gwen, Shannon and Katy for their brilliant feedback while test-knitting some of the harder designs. My more-than-heartfelt thanks go out to Susan and Sarah, my constant companions in fibery crime no matter where we are on the globe. To Maxine, many thanks for encouraging me, advising me and seeing me through my thesis. To Katie for her unending support and knitting vacations. To Benjamin, who sweeps up all the wool dust and gently puts stray balls back into their baskets. And to Jenni and Tonia at North Light Books, thank you for this wonderful opportunity.

Contents

Introduction 6
Where to Find Wool 8
Finding and Recycling Sweaters 10
Tools 16
Techniques 18
Planning a Project 36

HaTS ✹ 42

Little Flower Top Hat 44
Cupcake Hat 46
Wood and Water Hat 48
Blooming Tulips Hat 50
Lollipop Hat 52
Mountain Sunset Inside Out Hat 54
Berry Bramble Hat 56
Lake Reflects Trees Hat 58
Fresh-Cut Grass Hat 60
Forest Gnome Hat 62
Apple on the Tree Hat 64
Sweet Pea Hat 66
Root Vegetable Hat 68
Back Alley Hat 70
Snow Princess Hat 72

HeaDGear ✹ 74

All Things Grow Hat 76
Nautical Nellie Hat 78
1970s Ski Sweater Hat 80
Biker Hat 82
Daisy Helmet Hat 84
Yellow Bells Jester Hat 86
Twirly Girl Bonnet 88
Butterfly Pixie Bonnet 90
Daffodil Headband 92
Flapper Eyelet Headband 94
Fruit Punch Headband 96

mittens ❋ 98

Popsicle Mittens 100
Snow Day Mittens 102
Night Sky Wristers 104
Tree Bud Mitts 106
Communion Mitts 108

scarves ❋ 110

Moon over Waves Scarf 112
Snuggly Neck Scarf 114
Silky Smoke Ring 116
Flutter Neck Scarf 118
All-Star Scarf 120

Resources 122
Patterns 124
Index 127

Introduction

Welcome to my living room. Choose a mug or teacup and help yourself to the tea on the coffee table. Take a seat on the polka-dot couch or on one of the comfy chairs. Feel free to explore, to examine the posters, paintings and other artifacts from my journeys, or to browse the books on the shelves and in piles on the floor. Sip your tea and notice the baskets of yarn tucked into every corner. Half-finished projects pepper the room; two spinning wheels sit side by side next to a round basket full of colorful piles of wool and a mug full of double-pointed needles. If you want to knit, you've come to the right place—I have the supplies and support, and I give both willingly.

In many ways, I hope this book is like an extension of my living room: I want it to be a place you can enter, relax, drink tea and indulge in all things wool. I'll share some of my coziest patterns, and along the way I'll show you how to take your knitted items to the next level by transforming them into canvasses for artful stitching, buttons and other embellishments. Once you learn to add your own creative twist to hand-knit hats, mittens and scarves, you can make each item you create a unique work of art perfectly suited for you or its lucky recipient.

Within these pages, I hope to pass on my experience to you not only in the form of knitting and embellishing techniques, but also with the empowering knowledge that you can expand your knitting horizons and be creative in new ways. I want to push you beyond traditional crafting into artistic creation with interesting new approaches to yarns, textures, color combinations and embellishments. Soon you'll be warming yourself and those around you with your one-of-a-kind works of art!

WHERE TO FIND WOOL
... and why I believe you need a lot of it

First, I must confess that I am an accessory knitter. I love knitting small projects, and many of my yarn-obtaining habits are conducive to that knitting style. I do not need whole bags of wool. If I do happen to find a great deal on a bag of wool and buy it, I'll use it forever. I generally buy small quantities of yarn. One skein can be enough to make me happy for a very long while because there are so many combinations that I can get when combining new yarns with the yarns I already have. Don't worry if you're thinking right now that you need larger quantities of yarn—sweater recycling and yarn store sales will give you those. But for the accessories in this book, it is to the smaller quantities of yarn that we turn.

To me, wool is a perfect medium because it provides both the textures and the colors that my creative imagination revels in. I must admit that I have a rather large amount of yarn, but I can't imagine knitting without having so many options handy. I come from a painting background, so I am used to having a wide spectrum of colors at my disposal. Another good reason to have so much yarn around is that I can be generous with both my knowledge and my supplies when someone wants to learn to knit. One of my goals as a fiber artist is to spread and further the craft as much as possible. Providing support and materials is a great place to start.

There are several ways and places that I find yarn. I regularly shop for yarn at thrift stores. Shopping in thrift stores is good not only for the budget, but also for the world. When I shop at a thrift store, instead of buying something new, I am choosing to reuse something that someone else didn't want anymore to make something new. Another great reason to shop at thrift stores is to search for sweaters to recycle. (To learn how to turn a sweater into yarn for knitting, see *Finding and Recycling Sweaters* on page 10.) I enjoy taking something that had no thought or love in its making and creating something beautiful and useful from it. When I do this, I am saying "No" to the consumerism that goes along with so much of modern life and "Yes" to caring for our resources.

I also find that shopping at thrift stores stretches my limits as an artist. I often pick up yarns that I normally wouldn't buy in a regular yarn store, but because they're great bargains, I buy them anyway. Then, I have to think creatively to find the right projects for these yarns. Thrift stores are

also a great place to shop for fun embellishments such as buttons, tapestry wool and scraps of fabric for appliquéing. Don't give up if you don't find a treasure trove at the first thrift store you visit. You may have to poke around a bit before you discover a thrift store with yarn and other great finds.

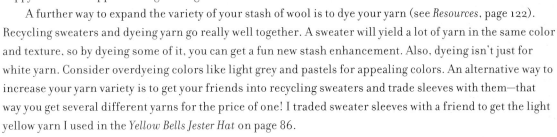

Although yarn from thrift stores and sweater recycling can be a large part of your stash, it generally won't be all of it. There are plenty of fun commercial yarns that I will grab a skein or two of whenever I can to regularly expand my color palette. Another benefit to buying commercial yarns is that there are many fibers available commercially, like angora and alpaca, that you may not find while thrifting. In addition, commercial yarn comes with a handy ball band that recommends gauge and needle size, which takes away the guesswork when working with a new yarn.

Another wonderful resource I've found for obtaining new-to-me yarn is former knitters. Don't underestimate the kindness of strangers. There are many, many people out there who used to knit, and you should graciously accept their gifts if you can use them, or if you know someone else who might use them. Usually, former knitters are just happy to see the supplies being used again and cleared out of their basements.

A further way to expand the variety of your stash of wool is to dye your yarn (see *Resources*, page 122). Recycling sweaters and dyeing yarn go really well together. A sweater will yield a lot of yarn in the same color and texture, so by dyeing some of it, you can get a fun new stash enhancement. Also, dyeing isn't just for white yarn. Consider overdyeing colors like light grey and pastels for appealing colors. An alternative way to increase your yarn variety is to get your friends into recycling sweaters and trade sleeves with them—that way you get several different yarns for the price of one! I traded sweater sleeves with a friend to get the light yellow yarn I used in the *Yellow Bells Jester Hat* on page 86.

If you want to go even further into the fiber arts, you can also try spinning your own yarn (see *Resources*, page 122). If you are not interested in spinning your own yarn, I encourage you to consider buying handspun or hand-dyed yarns from small businesses and independent artists (see *Resources*, page 122). Throughout this book, I knit with several handspun yarns from small yarn companies. Not only are these yarns beautiful, creative and a pleasure to knit with, but they also make you feel great for supporting a small business. I keep a basket full of small balls of handspun and hand-dyed yarns (mine and others) in a basket in my living room for daily inspiration.

Gathering supplies is a slow and cumulative process. Once you have a compatible collection, try to find the right places and projects for each of the yarns you have collected. Add a new yarn once in a while for creative inspiration. I always have a spurt of creativity right after I dye a new batch of recycled sweater wool. Throughout this book, you will see combinations not only of disparate colors, but also of textures and yarns. Often, my greatest inspiration comes from seeing yarns combined with whatever they land next to in the box or basket I'm keeping them in. I would like to encourage you to take a similar journey. Push yourself: Fill out your color palette, whether at a thrift store or a yarn store. Buy orange, just so you can look at it next to other colors. Buy crazy handspun yarn and mix it with some basic commercial wool.

Explore. Engage. Enjoy!

FINDING AND RECYCLING SWEATERS

As I mentioned, I love recycling sweaters. I enjoy salvaging something that may have been thrown away and giving it new life. Plus, I'm getting some good wool out of the deal for a killer price. Who can blame a girl?

When you thrift for sweaters, you're going to need to be smart. I have bought sweaters that were not good for recycling and I've learned from my mistakes. When you are shopping for sweaters to recycle there are several factors to consider: the condition of the sweater, the fiber content of the yarn, the type of seams and the gauge of the yarn.

CONDITION

When you shop for a sweater to recycle for knitting yarn, you want a sweater that isn't of questionable condition. A hole or two is fine, but remember that each hole means a break in the yarn. Several holes in a sweater means several small balls of yarn in your stash. This is also true of patterned sweaters. I often find patterns are not worth the time and energy required to free the wool, but these small balls of yarn may not be a bother to you. If the pattern is only on the front, it may be worth unraveling the sweater for the back and sleeves, which will result in large balls of yarn. Take into consideration how much wool you want or need from the sweater.

Wool that is nearly worn through may break easily when you are ripping out the sweater, or later when you are knitting. Check the elbows for wear and thinning. Felted sweaters are also no good. If you've ever accidentally thrown your favorite wool sweater in the washer and dryer, you have witnessed felting. In felted sweaters, the wool is fused together and cannot be unraveled. If a sweater seems shrunken or misshapen, it may have been felted. Check the seams to be sure, because the seams of a felted sweater will be fused shut. A sweater may also become felted in certain areas through normal wear—always check the seams around the armpits, where there is a lot of friction, and make sure the seams are loose enough to remove the sleeves from the sweater.

CONTENT

My very favorite fiber by and far is wool. Overall, I prefer yarns composed of 100 percent animal fiber or animal fiber blended with a little bit of nylon for strength. Although mohair is an animal fiber, I do not generally recycle sweaters with mohair content because the yarn is very difficult to unravel. Because of my personal preferences, I also tend to avoid synthetics. I will occasionally buy a sweater with up to 50 percent synthetic fiber if the yarn is fun and unique, but that's my cutoff point. You'll have to experiment with different yarns to establish for yourself what you are looking for.

If a sweater does not have a tag, it can be difficult to determine its fiber content. You may not want to buy a sweater or yarn unless you're reasonably sure of the contents. One way to determine the fiber content of yarn is a burn test. To burn test yarn, place a scrap of yarn in a fireproof container, carefully set the end on fire, let it burn for a few seconds and then blow it out. Wool and other animal fibers will self-extinguish and tend to smell like burning hair. Natural animal fibers also turn into ash as they burn. Most synthetics will melt or form a hard bead as they burn instead of producing ash. Some synthetics will self-extinguish and some will need to be blown out.

SEAMS

Another factor to consider when buying a sweater to recycle is its seams. If a sweater's seams are serged, the yarn has been cut at the end of each row, so if you try to take one apart, you'd only get short scraps of yarn. However, if a sweater is serged only on the top of the shoulders, you'll lose very little wool, so go for it! If the seams are serged all the way around the armholes, you will be able to retrieve the yarn from the front and back of the sweater up to the bottom of the armhole. One of my favorite thrift store finds was a horribly out-of-date Irish tourist knit. The beauty of the wool made retrieving as much yarn as I could worth the effort, even though the armhole seams were serged.

A sweater that is good for recycling will have seams that look like two columns of stitches traveling upwards side by side. If you gently pull apart the seam, you will be able to see the yarn used to sew up the sweater. Good seams will be easy to pull apart to expose the sewing thread or yarn.

You may also occasionally run across hand-knit sweaters on your thrift store expeditions. Although it is always sad to recycle a hand-knit sweater, sometimes it is the only way the sweater will get used. Just like commercial sweaters, hand-knit sweaters also fall out of style or fit poorly. If you plan on recycling a hand-knit sweater, know that they are not as predictable as machine-knit sweaters. It is also wise to know how hand-knit sweater construction generally works if you plan to undo someone else's work (see *Resources*, page 122).

SERGED SEAM
Since this sweater has serged seams, it cannot be recycled easily.

CROCHETED SEAM
The crocheted seam on this sweater will make it easy to recycle.

YARN GAUGES
From left to right: lace weight, fingering weight, sport weight, worsted weight, bulky weight and chunky weight yarns.

GAUGE

One of the things you'll be looking for in a thrifted sweater is a good gauge, and a good gauge completely depends upon what you want to make. For instance, if you want to knit a light lace shawl, a lace weight or fingering weight yarn will suit your needs. For a warm hat, however, you'll want a worsted weight or heavier weight yarn. The correct size of yarn always depends upon what you are going to do with the yarn. If you find a yarn that you fall in love with, but it is too thin, don't forget that you can also knit with the yarn doubled to mimic a heavier gauge.

To find the gauge of the yarn used in a sweater, find the number of stitches per inch (centimeter) in the knitted fabric. Take a ruler with you to the thrift store when you are sweater shopping. Lay the ruler on the knitted fabric so that it is parallel to the horizontal rows of knitted stitches. On stockinette fabric, each stitch will look like a V. Count the number of stitches that are in an inch (centimeter) of

fabric. Use the guide on page 123 to identify the gauge of the yarn. Be aware that sometimes yarn used in commercial sweaters may be misleading. The stitch count may tell you that the yarn is bulky weight, but that may be because the yarn is actually eight strands of lace weight yarn held together. Look closely at the sweater and study the characteristics of the yarn to make sure you can use it.

I often look for yarns with a gauge range from $3\frac{1}{2}$-7 stitches per inch (1-3 stitches per centimeter). My favorite yarn for accessories is worsted weight because it makes a fabric that is versatile and takes only a moderate amount of time to knit. Be sure to check each section of the thrift store when you are shopping. Often, women's clothing will be knit in a fine gauge or lack animal fibers, whereas men's clothing uses more worsted weight wool. Plus, a man's extra-large sweater gives much more yarn than a woman's small.

SWEATER DECONSTRUCTION

So, you've found a sweater that you'd like to recycle. It has good seams, not too much wear and a decent gauge. Now what?

The first thing you need to do is break the sweater down into its separate pieces along the seams. I once found a commercial sweater done entirely in the round with short row shaping, but generally commercial sweaters are composed of several pieces: the front, the back, the sleeves and sometimes a collar or hood. Turn the sweater inside out and take a closer look at the seams. Examine each to see how the sweater was put together. Most commercial sweaters I find are crocheted together. When the seams are crocheted, sometimes you just need to find the right yarn to pull and the entire seam will unravel. It's like magic.

A crocheted seam looks like a line of backstitching on one side of the seam and a column of Vs on the other side. The yarn used to seam the sweater often will be dyed to match the knitted fabric, but will be a smaller gauge than the knitting yarn. The crochet stitches of the seam are easy to see on a smooth stockinette fabric, but on a textured or ribbed sweater, it can be more challenging to find the seam yarn.

Find the end of the crocheted seam where the Vs are right-side up. This could be either at the top or the bottom of your seam. Slide one blade of your scissors under one of the crochet Vs close to the end of the seam, taking care not to pick up any of the yarn from the main body of the sweater. Cut both pieces of yarn making up the crochet V. Wiggle the fabric on either side of the cut seam to loosen it. Watch for the strand that you just cut to work its way out of the fabric. When you find the cut strand, pull on it and it should take out the crochet chain on the other side. If this doesn't work, make sure that you completely cut through the seaming yarn. If you did, pull the seam apart a bit more, because the seam may be slightly felted or the seaming yarn could be caught. Keep experimenting and fishing until you find the right strand to pull. If you are having difficulty, you can cut another V elsewhere on the seam and try again—even right below the V you just cut. I've been known to get frustrated and make another cut less than an inch away! Sweater ripping is not an exact science, but once you've taken apart one or two, you'll be a seasoned professional.

If you find a sweater that is not crocheted together, pull the seam apart to find the yarn used to sew the sweater together. Snip the seaming yarn and give the seam a good wiggle. If the seam unravels easily, pull the seaming yarn until the seam is completely unraveled. You can also seam rip or snip the entire seam if you are having difficulty unraveling it. On a few sweaters I've recycled, I found it easier to just firmly grasp the fabric on each side of the seam and rip the seam after the initial cut.

Don't be discouraged or panic if you cut the wrong yarn when trying to figure out a new sweater. I still do that sometimes. It just means you have one ball of yarn that is smaller than the others. Life will go on, and you'll still have plenty of beautiful, useful yarn.

CUTTING A CROCHETED SEAM
Slide one blade of your scissors under one of the crochet Vs close to the end of the seam, taking care not to pick up any of the yarn from the main body of the sweater. Cut both pieces of yarn that make up the crochet V.

Once you're done freeing up each section of the sweater, you are ready to unravel the yarn. Most commercial sweaters will be easiest to unravel from the top down. Select a sleeve from your sweater and look at its top edge. If the armhole was not serged, there will be another crochet chain or a row of bound-off knit stitches along the top (both will look like a row of Vs). Once you find the Vs there, cut the topmost one just as you did with the crocheted seam. Then, find the thread coming from inside of the V and pull. Usually that will be the only cut you'll have to make to start unraveling. If this method does not work for your sweater, you have several options. One is to find the end that is sewn in and figure out how the knitting is bound off. Undo the bound-off edge of the knitting and begin unraveling the yarn. Another option is to cut off the top row of knitted stitches and start unraveling the yarn from there. If things get too frustrating, I highly recommend taking your scissors to the knitting! If you have a sweater with a serged seam on top, you will need to cut off the first row of knitted stitches to be able to unravel the knitting.

As you unravel the sweater, wind the yarn into a ball; otherwise, the yarn will knot and you will have a mess on your hands. Wind the yarn into a loose ball with some squish to it. If you wind the yarn too tightly, you'll disrupt the structure of the yarn.

Since I sew in the ends of my yarn as I knit rather than knotting them together, I break the sweater yarn at any knot I come to and start a new ball of yarn. If you are comfortable with knots in your yarn, you can continue to wind the yarn into one ball as you come to any knots. More often than not, I get large balls of yarn from a sweater without running into knots. Sometimes, plied or multistranded yarns will have knots in only one ply or strand. If I run across that type of knot, I'll often ignore it as long as it is small. If a sweater is poorly made, there may several knots throughout the yarn. So far, this has happened to me only one time.

Once the entire piece of knitting has been unraveled, wind the yarn into a skein around the back of a chair or on a niddy noddy, a tool made for this purpose. Tie the skein in at least four different places with scrap yarn. Fill your

UNRAVELING KNITTED FABRIC

As you unravel the sweater, wind the yarn into a loose ball; otherwise, the yarn will knot and you will have a mess on your hands.

sink or a small washtub with room-temperature water. Without creating suds, add a small amount of soap or wool wash to the water. I like to use wool washes, such as Eucalan, even though they are a bit pricey, because I don't have to rinse them out. You can also use dish soap or a mild detergent (but not Woolite; it disrupts the wool fibers).

Place the skeined yarn on the surface of the water and allow it to submerge. Let the yarn soak for at least twenty minutes. If you are using soap or detergent, rinse the yarn twice to make sure all of the soap or detergent is removed. Be gentle with your fiber while rinsing, softly pressing and squeezing the yarn in clean room-temperature water to get the soap out. Do not run water directly onto the yarn. Once the yarn is rinsed, gently squeeze out what water you can, then roll the yarn in a towel to rid it of excess water. If you have access to a washing machine, skip the squeezing steps and run the yarn through the spin cycle in the washer. Be careful not to let the washer begin filling with water.

After most of the water is squeezed or spun out of the yarn, give the skein a few good whacks against a wall or your leg, then hang it up to dry. Some wool will come out of the bath fairly straight, but some will still have kinks in it. I usually knit with whatever I get at this point. If you want your yarn to be straight and it is not, you can weight the skein as it hangs drying. To weight your skein, put the hook of a hanger through the bottom of the skein and place a towel on the hanger. This is usually enough weight to pull the yarn straight. Be careful not to put too much weight on your yarn because its structure can be damaged.

Once the yarn is completely dry, you're ready to knit!

PREPARING YARN FOR WASHING
Wind the unraveled yarn into a skein around the back of a chair or on a niddy noddy. Tie the skein in at least four different places with scrap yarn.

TOOLS

The patterns in this book require very few tools, but there are a few items that you might find handy. I like to keep my knitting process simple, but the few tools I do have are well-loved and well-used.

KNITTING NEEDLES

Knitting needles are available in a wide variety of materials, including metal, wood, plastic and bamboo. I recommend trying a variety of needles to find the ones that suit you and your projects. To find out the recommended needle sizes for the yarn you're using, see the chart on page 123. Since small variations in size and gauge don't make a big difference in the accessories I enjoy knitting, I am able to be quite inventive about using the needles I have on hand, rather than buying needles in every size.

STRAIGHT NEEDLES are pointed at one end and have a stopper at the other end to keep stitches from sliding off. They are used to knit flat pieces of fabric, such as scarves.

DOUBLE-POINTED NEEDLES (DPNs) are pointed at both ends. Sold in sets of four or five, they are used to knit small projects in the round. I often use dpns to knit the top of a hat after it is too small to fit on a circular needle. I like the incredible silliness of trying on a hat while it is in progress with dpns sticking out of it. At the tops of hats, I don't worry too much about the size of the dpns matching the size of the circular needle I started the hat with. I think it makes very little difference to go up or down a size in either direction at the top of a hat.

CIRCULAR NEEDLES are joined together by a flexible cord. They can be used to knit projects in the round, but you can also knit flat pieces of fabric with circular needles. To knit a flat piece of fabric on a circular needle, simply turn your work when you reach the end of a row and work back in the other direction.

KNITTING NEEDLES
Shown from top to bottom: straight needles, double-pointed needles, circular needles.

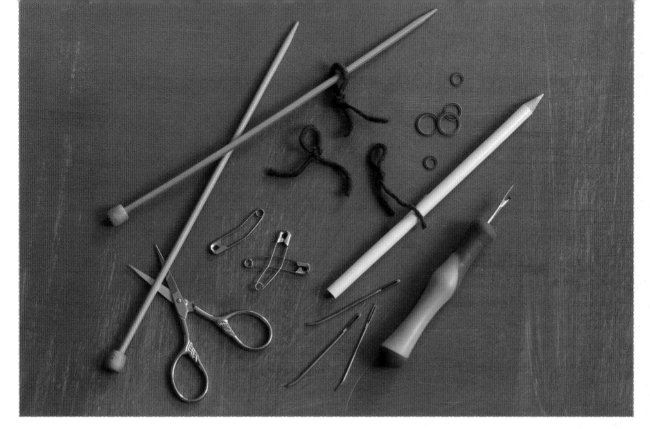

NOTIONS

Shown clockwise from top center: stitch markers, quilting pencil, seam ripper, tapestry needles, safety pins, scissors.

NOTIONS

I find that I need very few notions to keep me working happily along, but here are a few that make life easier.

STITCH MARKERS are rings used to denote a special place in your knitting. I find these especially useful to keep track of decreases in hats. There are many options for stitch markers—some knitters run little businesses that make fancy stitch markers, or you can buy simple plastic ones at any craft store. You can even use pieces of scrap wool that you have lying around, which is my preferred method. To make a scrap wool marker, fold a piece of scrap wool in half and tie a knot at the top, leaving a loop big enough for your knitting needle to fit through. Just remember that when you come to a marker, you need to slip it, not knit it!

SCRAP YARN is the lifesaver in any knitting kit. It can be used to create stitch markers, hold live stitches, create an afterthought thumb and more! I keep cans of scrap yarn in my knitting spaces for any knitting "emergency."

A QUILTING PENCIL or chalk can be used to mark an embellishment pattern on your knitted fabric. It will disappear once your project is washed.

SEAM RIPPERS are usually found in sewing kits. I use them while deconstructing sweaters to get at threads in hard-to-reach places and to help with cutting small pieces of yarn.

TAPESTRY NEEDLES have blunt tips and eyes big enough to thread yarn through. I use tapestry needles for embroidery, sewing in ends and performing Kitchener stitch.

SAFETY PINS or removable markers also help to mark areas in your knitting that need special attention. However, instead of sitting on the knitting needle and marking a place in your current row like a regular stitch marker, they rest on stitches in the knitted fabric.

CROCHET HOOKS may seem like unusual items to feature in a book on knitting, but you can use crochet hooks in so many ways: to create nice edges and fun borders, to embroider, and to catch dropped stitches.

Techniques

I'm always saddened to hear how frustrated some of my friends have become when learning how to knit. I think the solution is to find instructions that suit your learning style. If you can easily interpret diagrams and written instructions, the following pages should set you on your course. If not, there are many other avenues to look to for guidance and information, such as classes at your local yarn shop, knitting guild or group, knitting programs on television and DVD or instructional downloads from the Internet.

CASTING ON

There are several different methods that can be followed to cast on, and each one produces slightly different results. Here are two of the most common cast-on methods.

LONG-TAIL CAST ON

This is the most common way to cast on stitches. It might seem a little awkward to hold the yarn this way and hook the needle tip through each loop, but once you get the hang of it, you'll be amazed at how quickly the stitches add up. This technique creates a nice, clean cast-on edge at the bottom of your knitting.

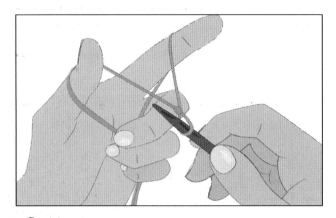

1. Position yarn

Make a slip knot, leaving a long tail (at least 4" [10cm] for every 1" [3cm] you'll be casting on). Slide the slip knot onto the needle with the long tail toward the front of the needle. Slide your thumb and index finger between the two strands of yarn. Wrap the long tail around your thumb and the strand still attached to the skein around your index finger. Grasp both strands with your remaining fingers.

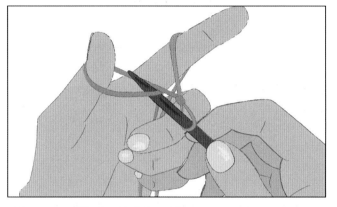

2. Bring needle through front loop

Slide the tip of the needle up through the loop of yarn wrapped around your thumb.

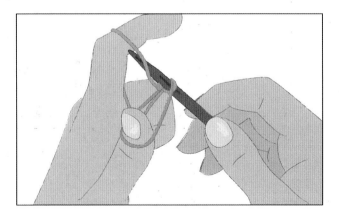

3. Catch second strand

Keeping the needle in the loop of yarn around the thumb, hook the needle behind the strand of yarn on the front of your index finger.

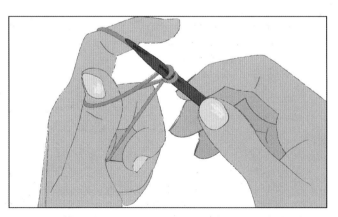

4. Draw back strand through front loop

Bring the yarn through the loop of yarn on your thumb, creating a second loop on your needle (the first cast-on stitch). Gently tug on the strands with thumb and index finger to tighten the cast-on stitch. Repeat to cast on the remaining stitches. Include the slip knot in your stitch count.

BACKWARD LOOP CAST ON

This is the simplest cast-on method to learn, but it does not provide the most stable edge. Use this cast-on method to close the body of a mitten or mitt into a round after the thumb stitches have been split from the knitting.

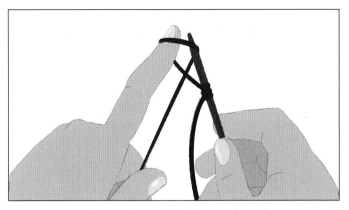

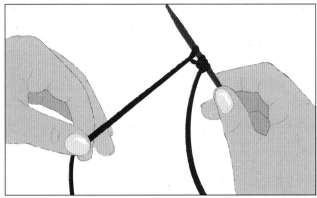

1. Create loop
Make a slip knot and slide it onto a knitting needle. Loop the working yarn around your index finger. Insert the tip of the knitting needle into the loop.

2. Tighten loop
Tighten the loop around your needle by gently pulling on the working yarn until the newly added stitch is snug on the needle. Repeat to cast on the remaining stitches. Include the slip knot in your stitch count.

KNITTING CONTINENTAL

When knitting continental, hold the yarn around your left fore-finger and dip the right-hand needle tip into it before making a stitch.

1. Position needles
With the working yarn wrapped over your left index finger, insert the right-hand needle into the first stitch on the left-hand needle from front to back. The right-hand needle should cross behind the left-hand needle.

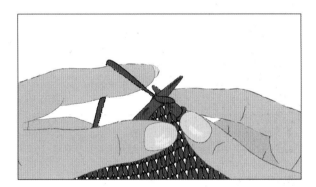

2. Wrap yarn
Bring the right-hand needle tip behind the yarn in front of your left index finger. The working yarn should be wrapped around the right needle tip counterclockwise.

3. Create new stitch
Dip the needle tip down and pull the wrapped yarn through the stitch on the left-hand needle. Bring the yarn up on the right-hand needle to create a new stitch, allowing the old stitch to slide easily off the left-hand needle. The new stitch remains on the right-hand needle.

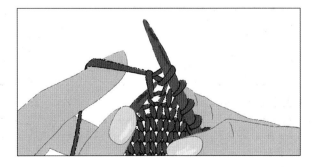

PURLING CONTINENTAL

Purling continental offers all the same advantages as knitting continental. Purled rows are easily distinguished by the raised wavy pattern.

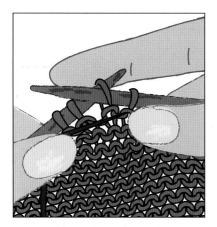

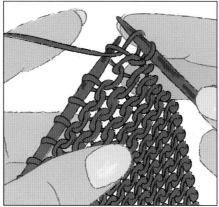

1. Position needles

With the working yarn in your left hand, slide the tip of the right-hand needle into the first stitch on the left-hand needle from back to front. The right-hand needle should cross in front of the left-hand needle.

2. Wrap yarn

Use your left hand to wrap the working yarn around the tip of the right-hand needle counterclockwise. Draw the right-hand needle back through the stitch on the left-hand needle, catching the wrapped working yarn with the tip of the needle. Bring the working yarn through the stitch on the left-hand needle.

3. Create purl stitch

Bring the yarn up on the right needle to create a new stitch, allowing the old stitch to slide off the left-hand needle. The new stitch remains on the right-hand needle.

For illustration purposes, the working yarn is shown held between the index finger and thumb. However, when working a row of purl stitches, the yarn should remain in the position shown in Step 2 to create proper tension.

JOINING STITCHES

When knitting in the round, stitches are cast on in the usual manner, and then joined with a knit stitch to form a circle.

JOINING WITH A CIRCULAR NEEDLE

Circular needles make knitting in the round almost effortless. Cast on, join the stitches and off you go!

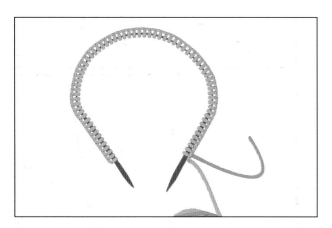

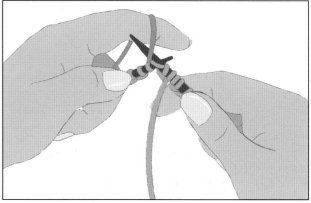

1. Cast on stitches

Cast on the required number of stitches and spread them evenly around the length of the circular needle. Lay the needle down on a flat surface with the working yarn on the right and the points of the needles facing you. Carefully straighten the cast-on row so that the bottom of each stitch is on the outside of the circular needle and none of the stitches are twisted over.

2. Join stitches

To join the stitches for working in the round, insert the right-hand needle into the first stitch on the left-hand needle from front to back. The right-hand needle should cross behind the left-hand needle. Pull the working yarn through to make a new stitch as usual.

JOINING WITH DOUBLE-POINTED NEEDLES

When you first start knitting with double-pointed needles, you may feel like you're playing a game of Pick-Up Sticks, but put a little work into learning this technique and you will be rewarded for the rest of your knitting life!

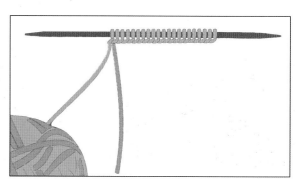

1. Cast on stitches

Cast on the required number of stitches onto one double-pointed needle.

2. Distribute stitches

Divide the cast-on stitches as evenly as possible among the double-pointed needles. If you are using a set of four double-pointed needles, distribute the stitches over three needles, leaving one needle for working. If you are using a set of five double-pointed needles, distribute the stitches over four needles, leaving one needle for working. When dividing the stitches, slip the stitches onto the new needle as if to purl; otherwise, your cast-on row will have twisted stitches. Lay the needles down on a flat surface with the working yarn on the right. Carefully straighten the cast-on row so that the bottom of each stitch is toward the inside of the needles and none of the stitches are twisted over.

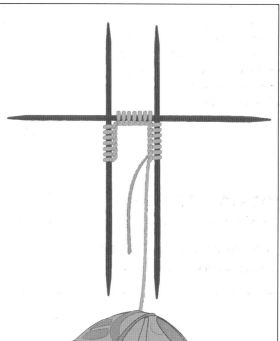

3. Join stitches

Hold the needle with the working yarn in your right hand and the needle with the first cast-on stitch in your left hand. Insert the tip of the free needle into the first cast-on stitch. Wrap the working yarn around the tip of the free needle and knit the first stitch as usual.

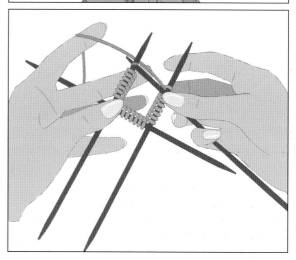

INCREASING AND DECREASING

Increasing and decreasing allow you to shape your knitting to any size. Eliminating stitches makes the piece smaller, and adding stitches makes the piece larger. Once you've familiarized yourself with these basic shaping techniques, you're ready to shape any of the patterns in the book.

KNIT TWO TOGETHER (K2TOG)

This technique really is as simple as it sounds. By placing your needle tip through two stitches instead of one, you knit the stitches together into a single stitch.

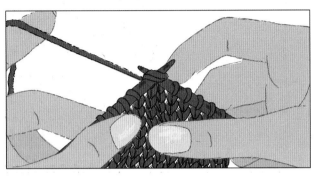

Slide the right-hand needle into two stitches together from front to back, as for a regular knit stitch. Knit the two stitches together as one stitch. This will lower your stitch count by one stitch. When the two stitches have been knitted together, you will see that the decrease leans to the right.

PASS SLIPPED STITCH OVER (PSSO)

This technique creates a left-leaning decrease that is usually paired with a k2tog to create a centered double decrease.

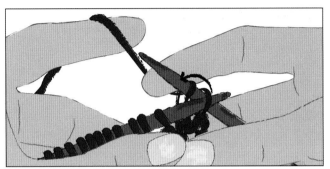

Insert the left-hand needle into the second stitch from the tip of the right-hand needle. Pull that stitch over the first stitch at the end of the right-hand needle and off of the right-hand needle. This will lower your stitch count by one stitch.

SLIP, SLIP, KNIT (SSK)

The SSK is the left-leaning symmetrical sister of k2tog that brings perfect shapely symmetry to your knitted piece.

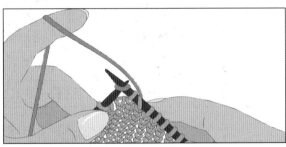

1. Slip stitches

Insert the tip of the right-hand needle into the first stitch on the left-hand needle as if to knit. Slip the stitch off of the left-hand needle onto the right-hand needle. Repeat with a second stitch.

2. Postion needles

Insert the left-hand needle into the fronts of both slipped stitches. The left-hand needle should cross in front of the right-hand needle. Wrap the working yarn around the right-hand needle, counterclockwise.

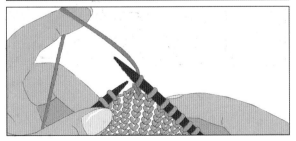

3. Knit stitches together

Knit the two stitches together as one stitch. This will lower your stitch count by one stitch. When the two stitches have been knitted together, you will see that the decrease leans to the left.

KNIT ONE FRONT AND BACK (KFB)

The title of this technique explains the process very clearly. By knitting a single stitch twice you create two stitches where there used to be one.

1. Knit into front of stitch

Slip the right-hand needle into the first stitch on the left-hand needle from front to back and knit the stitch as usual, but do not slip the stitch off of the left-hand needle.

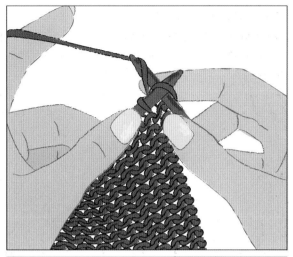

2. Knit into back of stitch

Insert the right-hand needle through the back of the same stitch and knit another stitch.

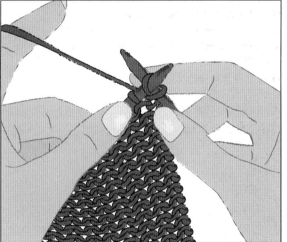

3. Create new stitch

Slide the old stitch off of the left-hand needle. The right-hand needle should now have two new stitches. This will increase your stitch count by one stitch.

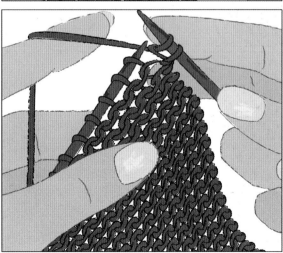

MAKE ONE LEFT (M1L)

This increase creates a defined line of stitches that slants to the left.

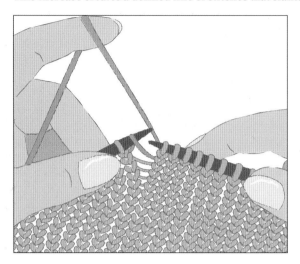

1. Lift bar
Bring the tip of the left-hand needle under the strand between stitches from front to back.

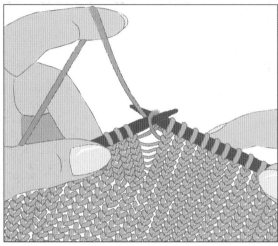

2. Position needles
Insert the tip of the right-hand needle through the back of the yarn sitting on the left-hand needle.

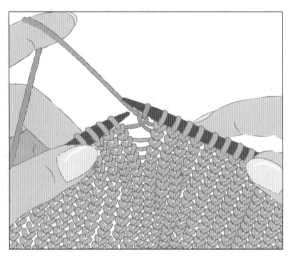

3. Knit new stitch
Knit this strand through the back loop to twist it. The right-hand needle should now have a new stitch. This will increase your stitch count by one stitch.

MAKE ONE RIGHT (M1R)

This increase creates a defined line of stitches that slants to the right.

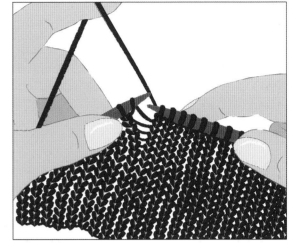

1. Lift bar
Bring the tip of the left-hand needle under the strand between stitches from back to front.

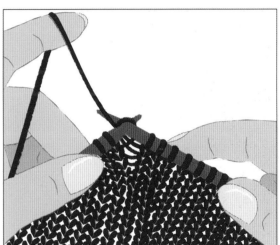

2. Position needles
Insert the tip of the right-hand needle through the front of the yarn sitting on the left-hand needle. The right-hand needle should cross behind the left-hand needle.

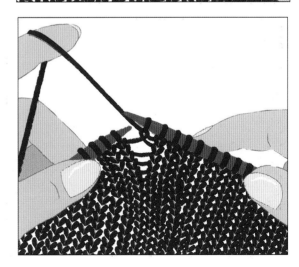

3. Knit new stitch
Knit this strand through the front loop to twist it. The right-hand needle should now have a new stitch. This will increase your stitch count by one stitch.

BINDING OFF

All good things must come to an end so they can be worn. Obviously, you can't just slip live stitches off your needle; if you did, your work would completely unravel. To finish off your knitting properly, you must bind off your stitches in one of the following ways.

TRADITIONAL BINDING OFF

This binding off process loops one stitch into another, stabilizing the edge of your work. It's very important to be aware of your tension while binding off. If you pull the stitches too tightly, you can pucker the top of your knitting and restrict its ability to stretch.

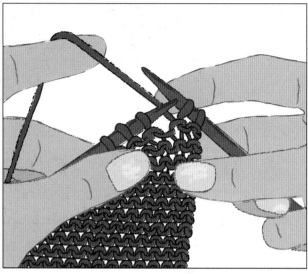

1. Knit two stitches
Knit the first two stitches in the row just as you would for a normal knitted row.

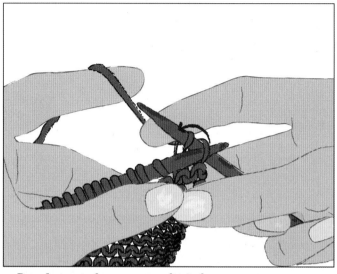

2. Pass first stitch over second stitch
Insert the left-hand needle into the first knitted stitch on the right-hand needle and pass it over the second knitted stitch on the right-hand needle.

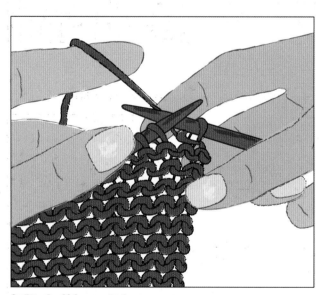

3. Bind off first stitch
One stitch will remain on the right-hand needle.

4. Bind off remaining stitches
To bind off the next stitch, knit one stitch (two stitches on right-hand needle), then pass the preceding stitch over the newly knitted stitch. Continue to knit one stitch and then pass the preceding stitch over it until you have bound off all the stitches. Cut the yarn and pull the tail through the final stitch.

THREE-NEEDLE BIND OFF

This technique is for binding off two pieces of knitting together to form a seam. Stitches are arranged evenly on two needles and a third needle is used to knit a stitch from each needle together and then bind them off.

1. Position stitches

Transfer your stitches evenly to two straight needles. Make sure the working yarn is at the pointed end of the needle. Holding the two needles together in your left hand, insert a third needle through the first stitch on each left-hand needle from front to back. The right-hand needle should cross behind both left-hand needles. Wrap the working yarn around the tip of the -right-hand needle.

2. Knit stitches

Knit the two stitches together as one stitch. Repeat Steps 1 and 2 to knit a second stitch.

3. Bind off first stitch

Insert one of the left-hand needles into the first stitch on the right-hand needle and pass it over the second knitted stitch on the right-hand needle. To bind off the next stitch, repeat Steps 1 and 2 to knit another stitch (two stitches on the right-hand needle), then pass the preceding stitch over the newly knitted stitch. Continue to knit one stitch and then pass the preceding stitch over it until you have bound off all the stitches. Cut the yarn and pull the tail through the final stitch.

CLOSING THE TOP OF CIRCULAR KNITTING

This technique is not technically a way to bind off stitches, but a way to finish your knitting and secure your stitches.

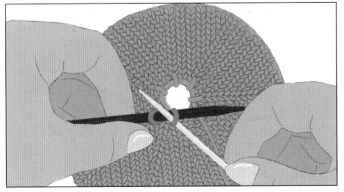

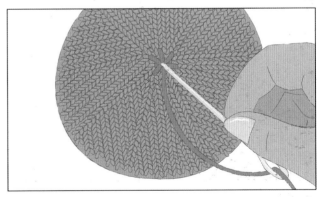

1. Slip stitches

After working the last round of the pattern, cut the working yarn, leaving at least a 6" (15cm) tail. Thread the yarn tail through the eye of a tapestry needle. Slip all stitches on the knitting needles onto the tapestry needle.

2. Tighten stitches

Pull the yarn tail through the stitches. Pull on the yarn tail and tighten the stitches until there is no gap at the closing point. Insert the tapestry needle into the center of the tightened stitches, pull the yarn tail through to the inside of the knitting and knot it. Weave the yarn tail into the wrong side of the knitting to secure it.

SEAMING WITH KITCHENER STITCH

Use Kitchener stitch any time you need to join two rows of knitted loops together. Kitchener stitch, when done correctly, looks like just another row of knitting and is as perfectly elastic as your knitted fabric.

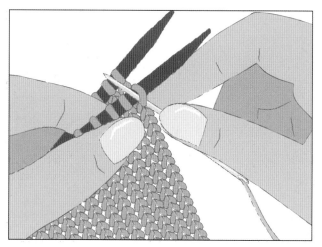

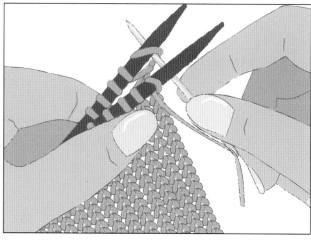

1. Make first set-up stitch

Transfer the stitches to be seamed evenly onto two straight needles. Make sure the working yarn is at the pointed end of the needle. Thread a tapestry needle with yarn. Hold the two needles together in your left hand with the wrong sides facing inward and the right sides facing outward. Insert the threaded tapestry needle into the first stitch on the left-hand needle closest to you as if to purl. Pull the tapestry needle through the stitch, leaving the stitch on the needle.

2. Make second set-up stitch

Insert the tapestry needle into the first stitch on the left-hand needle farthest from you as if to knit. Pull the tapestry needle through the stitch, leaving the stitch on the needle.

Steps 1 and 2 are done only to set up for seaming. Once these preparatory stitches are complete, the rest of the stitches will be seamed in the following pattern: knit, purl, purl, knit.

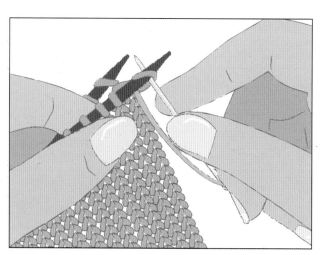

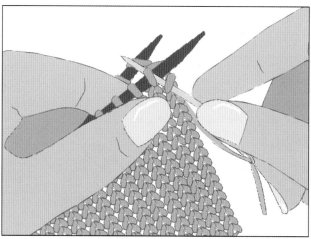

3. Slip stitch from front needle

Insert the tapestry needle again into the first stitch on the front needle, this time as if to knit, while slipping it off the end of the needle.

4. Continue grafting

Insert the threaded tapestry needle into the next stitch on the left-hand needle closest to you as if to purl. Pull the tapestry needle through the stitch, leaving the stitch on the needle. Pull the seaming yarn through the stitch, but do not excessively tighten the seam.

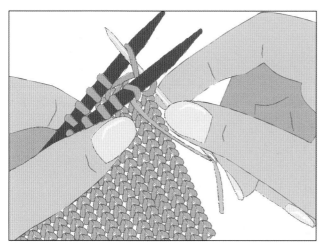

5. Slip stitch from back needle

Insert the tapestry needle again into the first stitch on the back needle, this time as if to purl, while slipping it off the end of the needle.

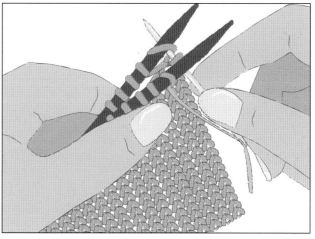

6. Continue grafting

Insert the threaded tapestry needle into the next stitch on the left-hand needle farthest from you as if to knit. Pull the tapestry needle through the stitch, leaving the stitch on the needle. Pull the seaming yarn through the stitch, but do not excessively tighten the seam.

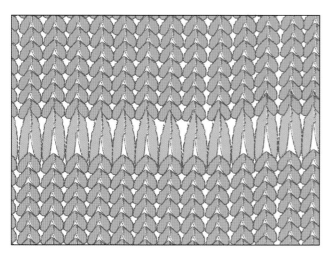

7. Finish grafting

Continue seaming until all of the stitches are grafted together. The seaming yarn will appear loosely woven between the two rows of grafted stitches.

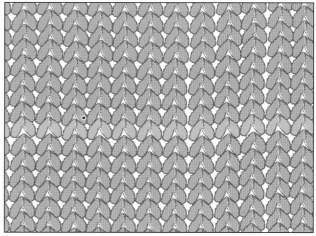

8. Adjust tension of seaming yarn

Lay the seamed fabric flat. Gently adjust the tension of the seaming yarn until it matches the tension of the knitted fabric. When the seaming yarn is properly tensioned, the seam should be invisible.

PICKING UP STITCHES

Making new stitches at the finished edge of a piece allows you to add new elements, such as earflaps, to your knitting. Picking up a stitch means you are creating new knitted stitches attached to the edge of the piece.

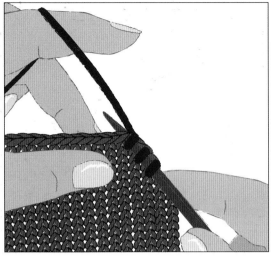

1. Position needle
Insert the tip of a knitting needle under a stitch on the finished edge of the knitted fabric. Be careful to pick up both strands of yarn from the stitch.

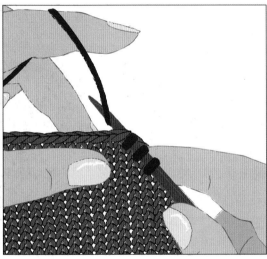

2. Wrap yarn
Wrap the working yarn around the tip of the needle counterclockwise, just as when knitting.

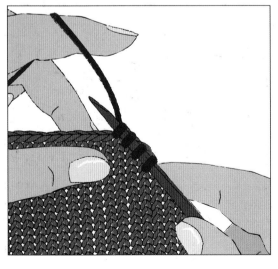

3. Create new stitch
Using the tip of the needle, pull the yarn through the knitted fabric, creating a new stitch on the needle. Continue picking up stitches until the appropriate number of stitches is on your needle.

KNITTING I-CORD

Use this technique to knit a three-dimensional piece without connecting the stitches. By simply sliding the stitches down to the other end of the double-pointed (or circular) needles, you force them to create a little tube. I-cords can be knitted in all different sizes and lengths and make handy ties, drawstrings, handles and even clever little topknots for stretchy hats.

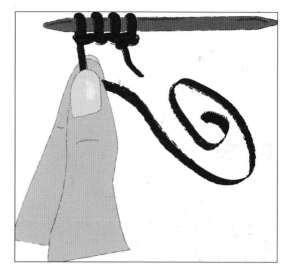

1. Cast on stitches
Cast on the required number of stitches onto one double-pointed needle.

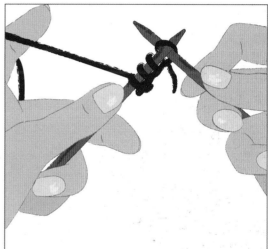

2. Prepare for first stitch
Slide the stitches on the double-pointed needle so that the first cast-on stitch is at the right-hand point of the double-pointed needle and the working yarn is to the left of the stitches. Insert another double-pointed needle into the first cast-on stitch.

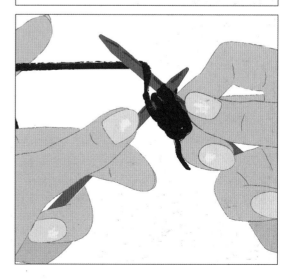

3. Knit I-cord
Pull the working yarn from the last stitch to the first stitch and knit. Knit all stitches in the first row. Instead of turning the needle when you finish a row as you would for regular knitting, simply slide all the stitches from the left point to the right point of the needle again. Do not turn your work at all while knitting I-cord. Keep pulling the working yarn behind the tube that forms to the first stitch in each row. After a few rows, you'll see the beginning of a knitted tube—without having purled a stitch, and without ever turning your work.

EMBELLISHING YOUR KNITS WITH STITCHING

The following techniques are traditional decorative stitches you can use to embellish your knits. Remember, though, that knitted fabric provides a much different base for stitching than stretched linen. Practice these stitches on knitted fabric to learn how to get the results you want.

SINGLE SATIN STITCH

Single satin stitches are straight stitches that are used to create free-form designs.

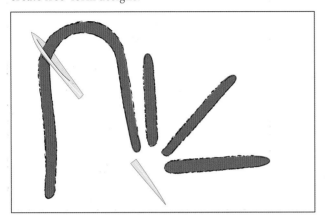

To form a single satin stitch, bring the needle up through the fabric at your desired starting point and down through the fabric at the end position of the stitch. Repeat as needed to finish your desired motif.

RUNNING STITCH

Running stitch is composed of a sequence of evenly spaced straight stitches of equal length.

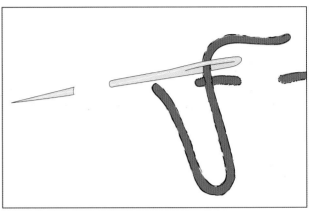

To embroider a line of running stitches, bring the needle up through the fabric at your desired starting point. Insert the needle into the end position of the first stitch in the series, then up through the fabric at the starting point of the next stitch. Repeat until the line of stitches is the length you desire.

OUTLINE STITCH

Outline stitch is composed of a series of stitches worked closely together to form the appearance of a twisting line.

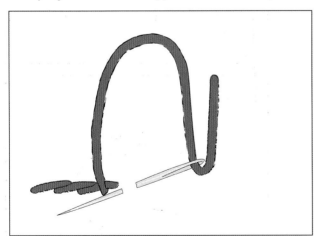

To embroider a line using outline stitch, working from left to right, bring the needle up through the fabric to start. Insert the needle down through the fabric a stitch to the right and bring it back up halfway along and below the preceding stitch. Continue to work by moving a stitch to the right, then along and below the preceding stitch until the line of stitches is the desired length.

BLANKET STITCH

Blanket stitch can be used as a decorative stitch or as an edging.

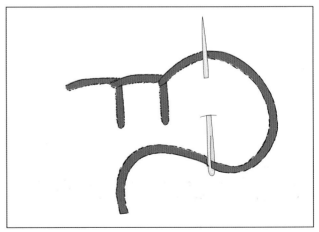

To embroider a piece using blanket stitch, begin by bringing the needle up through the fabric at your desired starting point. Insert the needle down through the fabric on a diagonal to the right of the starting point. Bring the needle back up through the fabric a stitch length to the right of the starting point. Loop the yarn under the needle, then pull the needle and yarn through the fabric and gently tighten the stitch. Continue to work by inserting the needle down on a diagonal and then up to the right of the previous stitch until the line of stitches is the desired length.

LAZY DAISY STITCH

Lazy daisy stitches are decorative stitches with the appearance of small flower petals.

1. Begin stitch

Bring the needle up through the fabric at your desired starting point. Insert the needle down into the fabric very close to the starting point.

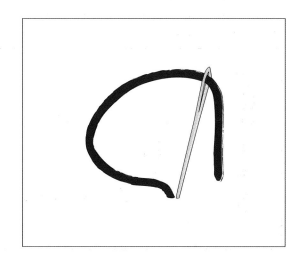

2. Continue stitch

Bring the needle back up through the fabric at the end position of the stitch. Loop the yarn under the needle.

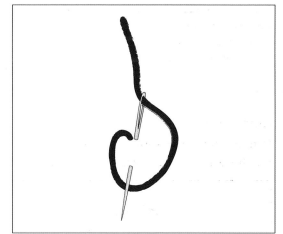

3. Complete stitch

Insert the needle down into the fabric on the other side of the yarn, forming a tiny stitch to hold the loop of yarn in place.

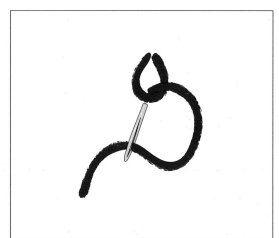

EMBELLISHING YOUR KNITS WITH CROCHET

Crochet can be used to embellish your knits as an edging or as a decorative stitch. These illustrations show working a crochet edging, but the same technique can be used to embellish the body of your knits by picking up stitches from the body of the knitted fabric rather than the edge.

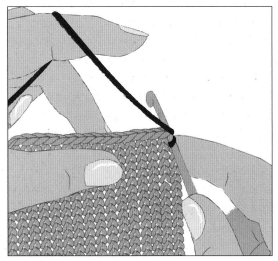

1. Insert hook
Make a slip knot and slide it over the crochet hook. Insert the crochet hook into the first stitch of the cast-on edge (or pick up one stitch from the body of the knitted fabric). Wrap the working yarn around the tip of the crochet hook clockwise.

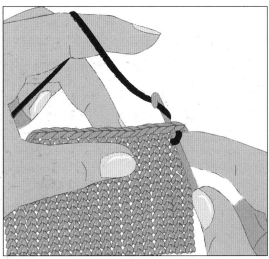

2. Create stitch
Pull the working yarn through the knitted fabric and the slip knot. Insert the hook into the next stitch in the cast-on edge (or knitted fabric). Wrap the working yarn around the tip of the crochet hook clockwise.

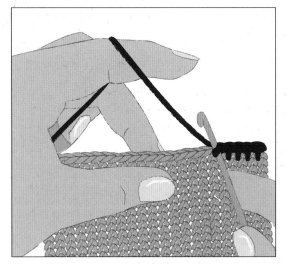

3. Continue chain
Pull the working yarn throught the knitted fabric and the loop of yarn from the previous stitch. Repeat Steps 2 and 3 until the edging or line of embellishment is complete. Cut the yarn and pull the tail through the final stitch.

CREATING DECORATIVE TASSELS

Cut a rectangle out of stiff cardboard. For a short tassel, I recommend cutting the cardboard to 2½" x 4" (6cm x 10cm), and for an average tassel, 4" x 6" (10cm x 15cm). Wrap the yarn for the tassel around the long side of the cardboard template approximately 25-40 times, depending on the thickness of the yarn and the desired fullness of the tassel. To secure the tassel, draw a strand of coordinating yarn, or multiple yarns, through the wrapped yarn at one end of the cardboard and knot it/them tightly. A braided cord or lanyard of yarn can also be used to secure the tassel for a more sophisticated look. Cut the yarn wrapped around the cardboard opposite the secured end. Using a coordinating yarn, tie the tassel off approximately 1" (3cm) below the secured end. After knotting, thread the yarn tails into the tassel with a tapestry needle. Trim the tassel to your liking. Use the yarn ends from the securing yarn to attach the tassel to a hat. If the hat is for an adult, you can just draw the tassel inside the hat and knot it. If the hat is for a child, I recommend sewing the tassel on.

CREATING DECORATIVE FRINGE

Cut a strand of yarn twice as long as the desired length of the finished fringe. Fold the yarn over and pull the looped end through the edge of the knitted fabric with a crochet hook. Thread the yarn tails through the yarn loop and pull tight. Repeat across entire area to be fringed. Once all the fringe is attached, trim the ends evenly. For a thick fringe, work with two or more strands of yarn held together and worked as one.

BLOCKING YOUR KNITS

Very few of the projects in this book need to be blocked to look their best. There are a few projects that I recommend blocking for, but the rest are your choice. Blocking can be helpful for several reasons. It evens out stitches and can fudge a size to be a bit bigger. Blocking works because animal-based fibers have memory—some more than others—and thus can still be molded and manipulated a bit after the garment is complete. Note that the laundering instructions even for commercial sweaters often recommend laying the garment flat and reshaping to dry.

To block a knitted garment, fill a sink or wash tub with tepid water and add a little bit of wool wash, mild detergent or dish soap. Try not to make suds, because they are hard to rinse out. Soak the knit garment for at least twenty minutes. If using a leave-in wool wash, you do not need to rinse; otherwise, rinse gently twice, gently pressing and squeezing the garment while it is completely submerged in the rinse water. After the final rinse, gently squeeze the excess water out of the garment and roll it in a towel, pressing to remove excess water. Lay the garment flat (I put it on a dry towel), reshaping it to the desired size and shape. If the garment needs more severe shaping, pin it out on carpet or a bed.

planning a project

While you can certainly create the patterns in this book just as they are shown, you can also easily customize them to your own personal tastes by selecting your own color palette and embellishments. My yarn selections and templates for all of the decorative stitching are provided to help you replicate these projects, but don't feel limited by my selections. If you're feeling adventurous, strike out on your own path!

COLOR THEORY

Much of this book is influenced by cross application from fine art to knitting because that is how I approach my work. My mother excels in fine art rather than craft, so much of my early training, including one of my bachelor's degrees was in fine art. Craft I found later, and I have always been thankful for my fine art training in my knitting life.

In *Where to Find Wool* on pages 8-9, I encouraged shopping outside of your comfort zone. In this section, I am going to encourage you to do something similar with color combinations. As I mentioned earlier, having a wide variety of yarn allows you to lay the balls of wool side by side and see if you like what happens. I am often unsure of what sort of project I want to make until I start laying colors alongside each other, switching them around and trying new combinations.

One problem with color theory is that when we talk about the colors, they are all the same intensity. Color theory is about pure colors that will always mix to give you other pure colors. Painting is not like that, and neither is knitting. I have fun considering the color wheel when I knit, but I am not bound to it. I do not in any way recommend using the color wheel for all of your knitting choices, but it's good to know how color works so that you can put a little theory to use when you start experimenting. Going with your gut is sometimes better than following the rules, but once in a while mixing up colors can teach you important lessons and help you overcome your color biases. Knitting truly becomes interesting to me when I start considering intensity, tone and tint along with basic color theory.

Complementary colors are opposite each other on the color wheel. When used in combination, complementary colors have quite a bit of pop because they are high contrast. The *Sweet Pea Hat* on page 66 shows this type of color interaction. The bright green embroidery stands out well against the pink knitted background.

Split complementary colors are a grouping of a particular color and the two colors that are on either side of its complement. Split complementary colors, when used at the same intensity, tend to be a bit less jarring than complementary colors of the same intensity.

Analogous colors are three colors grouped together on the color wheel. These colors work very well together and tend to be subtle and calm. The *Wood and Water Hat* on page 48 is a great example of how analogous colors interact.

Monochromatic colors are different shades of the same color in a spectrum of tints (white added) and tones (black added), often referred to as pastels, brights and darks. An example of this type of color interaction is the *Lollipop Hat* on page 52. For this hat I matched yarns in different shades of orange. The result is a subtle hat with a little bit of flair.

Yarn arranged by color in the order of a color wheel.

CHOOSING COLORS

There is an infinite number of ways to combine colors in your knits. When you are planning a project, consider details such as shape, embellishments and, most important, the wearer.

SHAPE

How I arrange the colors in my knits always depends upon the shape of the project. I like stripes on nearly everything, but if I'm going to show off a delicate shape, I may opt for more subtle striping. With hats, your decisions about color might be affected by what sort of decreases you use, whether the hat has earflaps or not, or the sort of brim you've chosen. The brim is especially important. It surrounds the face, and on adult hats it is the most visible part of the hat. With that said, make sure to consider the hat as a whole when you are selecting colors—it may even help to do a color drawing before you begin.

EMBELLISHMENT

Sometimes, your project may be designed around an embellishment you wish to use. In that case, arranging your colors could depend totally upon what sort of embellishment you have in mind and what will best emphasize it.

WEARER

This very well may be the driving force behind all of your design decisions. For example, my color choices vary as to whether the project is for a child or an adult. When you are designing, consider what the intended wearer likes and is likely to wear. My usual style of design is to work organically, creating as I go, but when I knit for a particular person, I often plan much of the project out ahead of time while consulting the recipient..

ARRANGING COLORS

Once you have chosen your colors, you need to decide how to arrange them. My favorite color-arranging techniques fall into four categories, as you will see in the projects section: color blocks, stripes, contrasting accents and single color.

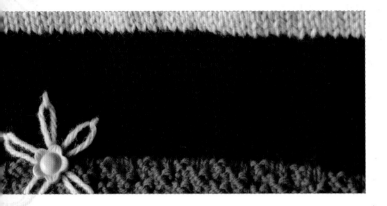

COLOR BLOCKS

These projects feature long, nonrepeating sections of color. I think that this combination works particularly well for small, square hats, like the *All Things Grow Hat* on page 76 and the *Daisy Helmet Hat* on page 84.

STRIPES

I use stripes on projects of every size and shape. If you like stripes, I suggest trying many variations. Each gives a totally different feel. Stripes of different sizes and shades, like those found on the *Nautical Nellie Hat* on page 78, create a bold, graphic look. Evenly spaced stripes are visually neat and tidy, like the *Biker Hat* on page 82. Subtle stripes, such as those used on the *Forest Gnome Hat* on page 62 and the *Little Flower Top Hat* on page 44, create yet another effect. I love the feeling of endless possibilities that working with stripes gives me.

CONTRASTING ACCENTS

These projects are mostly worked in a single color with an additional color added for contrast. Many of my hats have the brim in one color and the rest of the hat in another color. I often use this arrangement on a hat that I plan to embroider using the brim as a baseline, or when I love two wools together and have only a small bit of one of them. I also think that it gives the hat just a bit more punch than a single-color hat if I decide not to do too much embroidery on it. The *Snow Princess Hat* on page 72 features contrasting accents.

SINGLE COLOR

I make single-color projects primarily as a background to embroider and embellish on. The embellishment visually draws more attention if the knitted background is not distracting. I wanted the detailed embroidery on the *Apple on the Tree Hat* on page 64 to be the focus of the hat, so I knitted the hat in a single color. For projects such as this, most of my creative energy goes into embellishment alone.

EMBELLISHING

When it comes to embellishing, you once again have caught me looking at my knitting as if it were painting. When I finish knitting a garment, I analyze whether it is a balanced, whole, finished item, or if it needs something more. Sometimes that something more is as simple as a tassel, and sometimes it is as complex as an embroidered vignette. Look at your own knitted items: What do the colors and the shapes you have created inspire you to think about?

I have developed my own language of images that is very personal to me. These images are inspired by many things, including artistic movements, poetry, literature and my surroundings and experiences. Allow yourself to be inspired by what is around you to create your own set of images. Try many different things until you find yourself at home with your own vocabulary of shapes and forms to draw upon.

A quick look through the projects in this book will show you that when it comes to embellishing, I am obviously biased toward embroidery and buttons. Most of the information I will pass on to you concerns embroidery, but many of the rules and guidelines I use for embroidery, such as placement and color theory, can be applied to other embellishments as well.

The list of items that can be used to embellish knitting goes on and on, and I suggest that you try to incorporate any elements that interest you, as long as whatever you choose will not get in the way of the wearer, break easily, or pose a choking hazard if the recipient is a baby. Explore what captures your imagination.

DECORATIVE STITCHING

I consider myself a guerilla embroiderer. I started embroidering on hats and other accessories when I had no idea what I was doing. I learned most of what I know by putting the needle to the wool and starting to stitch. The stitches I use are illustrated on pages 32-33. I am satisfied with these, but if you are not, there are many embroidery stitch guides available to inspire you.

I must warn you that you will not learn everything you need to know from embroidery books, because stitching on knitting is different from other embroidery. Linen stretched in a hoop can be controlled and embroidered with perfect little stitches and lovely straight lines. When you embroider on knitting, the surface of the fabric will vary wildly from piece to piece.

For this sort of creative endeavor, you need to learn to go with the flow. Practice embroidering on knitted fabric until you are able to get what you want. Experiment and see what different yarns and stitches do on different surfaces. I rip embroidery out on a regular basis when it either doesn't work with the project or isn't doing what I want it to do. Feel free to start over.

To make life easier on yourself while you are learning to embroider on knitted fabrics, choose simple shapes or symbolic shapes that are easily recognized, such as trees. Consider abstract embroidery patterns rather than pictures. Try to remember that the design you embroider is not everything; there's also the interaction between the textures and colors of the embroidery yarn and the knitting yarn.

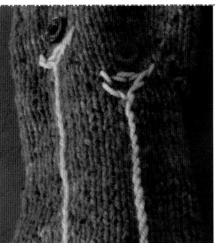

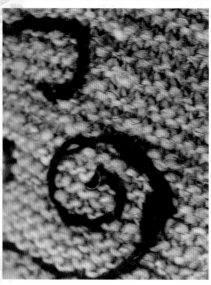

The first thing I do when I start embroidering on my knitting is choose the embroidery yarn. I have two large cans full of scrap yarn that I raid first. I lay different colors of yarn on the garment and think about the possible color interactions between the embroidery and the knitting (see Color Theory, page 36). I also consider contrasting yarn textures and weights. The embroidery on the *Forest Gnome Hat* on page 62 is a good example of several yarn textures and weights being used together. If the yarn you choose is the perfect color, but not the right weight, you can double it for thicker embroidery lines, or you can remove plies from multi-ply yarns for thinner embroidery lines. Once you have selected a yarn, thread your tapestry needle and start playing!

Placement is one of the most important parts of embellishment. The placement of your embellishments needs to make sense to the viewer. If you are embroidering something that makes sense sitting on its own, that is abstract or decorative, and that doesn't need a specific ground to sit on, you have more freedom in placement. Examples of this type of embroidery include the hearts on the *Popsicle Mittens* on page 100 and the snowflake on the *Snow Princess Hat* on page 72. Because these are independent designs, they work very well on their own.

On the other hand, if you are going to embroider something like a tree or a plant, consider some of the rules of painting. Although I do not insist that you need a shadow (although some shading on the object itself may be nice), you do need to make sure that your figure is grounded. If I am embroidering on a hat, for example, I often use the brim as the ground, or sometimes, I put my own ground in, working a line of stitches under the object. A contrasting brim emphasizes the idea of a horizon line, with which I like my landscape embroidery to interact. If you choose to make a landscape setting, make sure that it will visually make sense to the people looking at it. The brim area can also be embellished on its own, as I did on the *Root Vegetable Hat* on page 68.

Because you are working on a three-dimensional surface, you have the freedom to carry your embroidery around the sides and back of the garment, like I did on the *Snow Day Mittens* on page 102. In contrast, small embellishments can also be effective because they create a focal point, such as the embroidery on the *Nautical Nellie Hat* on page 78. You can also create embellishments that make the most of the natural shapes in your knitting, such as the *Little Flower Top Hat* on page 44 and *Lollipop Hat* on page 52, which both feature embroidery based on the decrease lines on the top of the hat.

These guidelines have helped me to create embellishments that I find visually pleasing, but they may not suit your taste. Break my rules and maybe you'll be the next Picasso or Pollock of the embellishing world.

FITTING AND SIZING HATS

It never fails to amaze me when I sell my hats at craft fairs how the shape and color of a hat often trump size for the buyer. Repeatedly I have sold child-sized hats to adults and they have walked away, wearing the hat, as happy as can be. It always makes me shake my head and smile. This is a good thing to remember and to take into account when you are knitting something you either don't like or are ambivalent about—there will always be someone who will treasure it. Hats do not need to have an exact fit. For that reason, I rarely make gauge swatches anymore when making hats. I cast on and knit, and if a couple of inches into knitting it seems to be the wrong size, I'll rip it out.

There are several things to take into account when knitting to fit your head (or someone else's). Some hats look great snug, while others look better oversized. Some look best stretched out so you can see the design. The patterns in this book are sized based on my opinion as to which fit is best for the design, but you, of course, may adjust according to your own taste. For instance, the *Forest Gnome Hat* on page 62 fits my head, but I think it looks much cuter on a child's head. When choosing the size to knit from the patterns in this book, measure around the largest part of your head. Determine how you'd like your hat to fit and select the size that will provide that fit. For instance, if you have a head with a 21" (53cm) circumference, and you like your hats to fit snugly, the size small *Wood and Water Hat* on page 48 may be for you with a brim circumference of 19" (48cm). However, if you are looking for a hat that will settle comfortably on your head and won't flatten your hair, you may want to try the size large, which has a 22½" (57cm) circumference.

Each of the hat patterns in this book has been sized using standard stitch count increases. To increase the size of a hat beyond the options already provided, simply find the standard stitch count increase used and add that number of stitches to the cast-on amount once for every size you wish to increase the pattern.

For example, the *Little Flower Top Hat* pattern on page 44 begins by casting on 80 stitches for a child's size small. For a child's size medium hat, the cast-on amount is 88 stitches, and for the child's large the cast-on amount is 96 stitches. To find the standard stitch count increase used in this hat pattern, subtract the number of stitches cast on for the medium size hat from the number of stitches cast on for the large hat; you could also subtract the number of stitches cast on for the small size hat from the number of stitches cast on for the medium size hat (96 stitches - 88 stitches = 8 stitches; 88 stitches - 80 stitches = 8 stitches).

From these calculations, you can see that the standard stitch count increase between sizes is 8 stitches for this pattern. To make a hat that is an adult's size small, add one standard stitch count increase to the number of stitches required for the child's size large. For this example, you would add 8 stitches + 96 stitches = 104 stitches.

Continue to follow the knitting pattern, paying attention to any operations that vary for the different sizes. Continuing with the *Little Flower Top Hat*, once you cast on, you knit a ribbed brim. The height of the ribbed brim varies between sizes by ¼" (6mm) (1¼" - 1" = ¼" [32mm - 26mm = 6mm]). For your adult's size small hat, you would add ¼" (6mm) to the ribbing measurement for the child's size large hat (1¼" + ¼" = 1½" [32mm + 6mm = 38mm]).

You would then continue on with the body of the hat, the height of which also varies according to size. Following the standard differences between each hat size (5½" - 4¾" = ¾" [14cm - 12cm = 2cm]), you would add ¾" (2cm) to the body measurement of the child's size large hat for an adult's size small hat (5½" + ¾" = 6¼" [14cm + 2cm = 16cm]).

The decrease section of this hat is the same for each of the child's sizes, and will also be the same for the adult's sizes: K6, k2tog. Working these decreases as instructed will result in 13 remaining stitches for an adult's size small hat. These remaining stitches will again be decreased following the same pattern as the child's size hats, resulting in 7 stitches that can then be bound off to finish the hat.

These instructions can also be reversed to resize an adult's hat to a child's size, subtracting instead of adding the standard stitch count increase of the pattern to reduce the size of the finished hat to a child's size.

Hats

The basic hat shape is a cylinder with one open end and one closed end, but there are endless variations within these guidelines. In this chapter we'll explore the many different hats you can create when you vary certain elements of the basic hat by adding increases, decreases, earflaps and more.

Each of the hats in this chapter is cast on at the brim. The brim is an important piece of a hat's design because it surrounds the face, making it a focal point. You'll find several different brim options throughout these patterns, including the ribbed brim of the *Wood and Water Hat* on page 48, the rolled brim of the *Mountain Sunset Inside Out Hat* on page 54, and the textured brim of the *Berry Bramble Hat* on page 56.

After the brim has been completed, the main body of the hat begins. At this point, stocking hats and beanies are worked even over the same number of stitches until the hat is the proper height to begin decreasing. However, there are several ways to add more shaping to the body of your hat. For a tamlike hat, the number of stitches can be increased, causing the body of the hat to flare out like the *Root Vegetable Hat* on page 68. You can also create a flare by switching to yarn in a different weight, as in the *Cupcake Hat* on page 46.

Shaping effects can also be created by the decreases you select for your hats. The top of a hat can be softly rounded, like the *Little Flower Top Hat* on page 44, gently pointed, like the *Lollipop Hat* on page 52, or dramatically different, like the *Forest Gnome Hat* on page 62. No matter what your taste, there is a hat top for you in these patterns!

Even after you bind off the last stitch of your hat, you have even more options. You can add earflaps like those on the *Lake Reflects Trees Hat* on page 58, and, of course, there is always embellishment. Who knew you could be so creative with such a simple shape?

Little Flower Top Hat

I keep a stash of small quantities of Mountain Colors yarns on hand because their dye palette is so different from my own. The location of their dye shop is only an hour from my hometown, so they are also close to my heart for that reason. Just a little bit of hand-dyed yarn can spruce up any hat, whether it is used for the knitting or the embellishment. One fun thing I like to do with embroidery is to play with what occurs naturally in the knitting pattern, from the brim ribbing to the decreases. On this hat, I used the petal-like nature of the decrease lines at the top of the hat to make a flower with my embroidery. This embellishment is perfect for a child's hat, but I don't think I would use it on an adult hat, because we so rarely see the tops of adult heads!

sizes

Child S (M, L)

finished measurements

Circumference: 16 (17½, 19¼)" 41 (44, 49)cm
Height: 6 (6¾, 7½)" 15 (17, 19)cm

yarn

Approximately 10 (13, 16) yards 9 (12, 15)m
worsted weight 100% wool yarn (A)
Approximately 10 (13, 16) yards 9 (12, 15)m
worsted weight 100% wool yarn (B)
Approximately 55 (65, 80) yards 50 (59, 73)m
worsted weight 100% wool yarn (C)
Small amounts of 100% wool yarn in 2 colors
for embellishment
*Shown: thrifted oddments, Mountain Colors
mill end*

needles

16" (40cm) US 7 (4.5mm) circular needle
Set of US 7 (4.5mm) dpns

*If necessary, change needle size to obtain
correct gauge.*

notions

Quilting pencil or chalk
Stitch markers
Tapestry needle

gauge

18 sts and 28 rows = 4" (10cm) in St st

knitting skills

k2tog [knit 2 together]: Dec by knitting 2 sts
tog as 1 st (see page 22)

embellishment skills

Outline stitch (see page 32)
Lazy daisy stitch (see page 33)

KNIT

STRIPE PATTERN

1 rnd yarn B

5 rnds yarn C

Do not cut color not in use, but carry it up the inside of the work.

BRIM

With circular needle and yarn A, CO 80 (88, 96) sts. Join for working
in the rnd, being careful not to twist sts. Place marker for beg of rnd,
if desired.

RND 1: *K2, p2; rep from * to end.

Rep Rnd 1 until piece measures ¾ (1, 1¼)" 2 (3, 3)cm from cast-on edge.

Change to St st and Stripe Patt and work even until piece measures 4 (4¾,
5½)" 10 (12, 14)cm from cast-on edge.

CROWN DECREASES

When knitting on the circular needle becomes uncomfortable, switch
to dpns.

NEXT RND: *K6, k2tog, pm; rep from * to end—70 (77, 84) sts.

Knit 1 rnd.

NEXT RND: *Knit to 2 sts before marker, k2tog; rep from * to end—60
(66, 72) sts.

Rep last 2 rnds 5 times more—10 (11, 12) sts.

NEXT RND: Knit 0 (1, 0), *k2tog; rep from * to end—5 (6, 6) sts.

Cut yarn, leaving a 6" (15cm) tail. Use tapestry needle to thread tail
through rem sts, pull tight and fasten off. Weave in ends.

EMBELLISH

Using the decrease lines at the top of the hat as a guide, transfer the
embellishment pattern below to the knitted fabric with a quilting pencil
or chalk. Using wool yarn and a tapestry needle, stitch the outer flower
petals using outline stitch. Create the inner petals with lazy daisy stitches.

Pattern | *enlarge template by
200% to bring to full size*

— — — decrease line

———— outline stitch

lazy daisy stitch

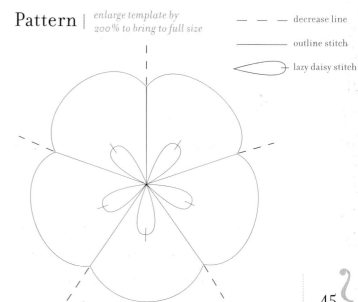

Cupcake Hat

This sweet hat is worked in two thicknesses of worsted weight yarn. The thicker yarn is used in the top of the hat to make it flare out slightly, like the top of a cupcake. Some simple embroidery and a round of purl stitches draw together the pink and red yarns. When I'm designing a new hat, I usually finish the knitting and then think about what embellishments the hat needs. For me, this hat was complete with just the simple stitching.

SIZES

Adult S (M, L)

FINISHED MEASUREMENTS

Circumference: 19 (21, 22½)" 48 (53, 57)cm
Height: 7½ (7½, 8½)" 19 (19, 22)cm

YARN

Approximately 45 (50, 55) yards 41 (46, 50)m
worsted weight 100% wool yarn (A)
Approximately 70 (80, 90) yards 64 (73,
82)m heavy worsted or Aran weight 100%
wool yarn (B)

*Shown: recycled sweater yarn, Peace
Fleece Worsted*

NEEDLES

16" (40cm) US 7 (4.5mm) circular needle
Set of US 7 (4.5mm) dpns

*If necessary, change needle size to obtain
correct gauge.*

NOTIONS

Stitch markers
Tapestry needle

GAUGE

20 sts and 32 rows = 4" (10cm) in St st with
yarn A
18 sts and 26 rows = 4" (10cm) in St st with
yarn B

KNITTING SKILLS

k2tog [knit 2 together]: Dec by knitting 2 sts
tog as 1 st (see page 22)

EMBELLISHMENT SKILLS

Running stitch (see page 32)

KNIT

With circular needle and yarn A, CO 96 (104, 112) sts. Join for working
in the rnd, being careful not to twist sts. Place marker for beg of rnd,
if desired.

RND 1: *K2, p2; rep from * to end.

Rep Rnd 1 until piece measures 1 (1, 1)" 3 (3, 3)cm from cast-on edge.

Change to St st and work even until piece measures 2¾ (2¾, 2¾)" 7 (7,
7)cm from cast-on edge.

Change to yarn B. Purl 1 rnd.

Continue in St st until piece measures 6 (6, 7)" 15 (15, 18)cm from
cast-on edge.

CROWN DECREASES

When knitting on the circular needle becomes uncomfortable, switch
to dpns.

NEXT RND: *K6, k2tog, pm; rep from * to end—84 (91, 98) sts.

Knit 1 rnd.

NEXT RND: *Knit to 2 sts before marker, k2tog; rep from * to end—72
(78, 84) sts.

Rep last 2 rnds 5 times more—12 (13, 14) sts.

NEXT RND: Knit 0 (1, 0), *k2tog; rep from * to end—6 (7, 7) sts.

Cut yarn, leaving a 6" (15cm) tail. Use tapestry needle to thread tail
through rem sts, pull tight and fasten off. Weave in ends.

EMBELLISH

Embroider along the top of the ribbing at the brim of the hat using
running stitch. Make each stitch as wide as a rib.

Wood and Water Hat

In designing this project, I wanted to create a hat that would flatter either a man or a woman. I started by choosing blue and green tones for the knitting and embellishments. I felt this was a good start, but I find men to be very picky when it comes to hats. For that reason, I am eternally in search of embroidery and button combinations that men will wear. The tree design I've used here is my most popular embroidery design for men so far, but I am still always looking for fresh inspiration.

sizes

Adult S (M, L)

finished measurements

Circumference: 19 (21, 22½)" 48 (53, 57)cm
Height: 7½ (7½, 8½)" 19 (19, 22)cm

yarn

Approximately 55 (60, 65) yards 50 (55, 59)m
worsted weight 100% wool yarn (A)
Approximately 45 (50, 60) yards 41 (46, 55)m
worsted weight 100% wool yarn (B)
Small amount of 100% wool yarn for
embellishment
*Shown: recycled sweater yarn, thrifted
oddments*

needles

16" (40cm) US 7 (4.5mm) circular needle
Set of US 7 (4.5mm) dpns
*If necessary, change needle size to obtain
correct gauge.*

notions

Quilting pencil or chalk
Stitch markers
Tapestry needle
1 ½" (13mm) button

gauge

20 sts and 28 rows = 4" (10cm) in St st

knitting skills

k2tog [knit 2 together]: Dec by knitting 2 sts
tog as 1 st (see page 22)

embellishment skills

Outline stitch (see page 32)

KNIT

STRIPE PATTERN

10 rnds yarn A

10 rnds yarn B

Do not cut color not in use, but carry it up the inside of the work.

BRIM

With circular needle and yarn A, CO 96 (104, 112) sts. Join for working in the rnd, being careful not to twist sts. Place marker for beg of rnd, if desired.

RND 1: *K2, p2; rep from * to end.

Rep Rnd 1 until work measures 1 (1, 1)" 3 (3, 3)cm from cast-on edge.

Change to St st and work even in Stripe Patt until piece measures 6 (6, 7)" 15 (15, 18)cm from cast-on edge.

CROWN DECREASES

When knitting on the circular needle becomes uncomfortable, switch to dpns.

NEXT RND: *K6, k2tog, pm; rep from * to end—84 (91, 98) sts.

Knit 1 rnd.

Next rnd: *Knit to 2 sts before marker, k2tog; rep from * to end—72 (78, 84) sts.

Rep last 2 rnds 5 times more—12 (13, 14) sts.

NEXT RND: Knit 0 (1, 0), *k2tog; rep from * to end—6 (7, 7) sts.

Cut yarn, leaving a 6" (15cm) tail. Use tapestry needle to thread tail through rem sts, pull tight and fasten off. Weave in ends.

EMBELLISH

Transfer the embellishment pattern below to the knitted fabric with a quilting pencil or chalk. Using wool yarn and a tapestry needle, stitch the embroidery pattern using outline stitch. Sew on button where indicated.

Pattern | *enlarge template by 167% to bring to full size*

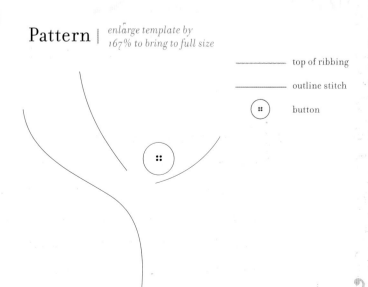

——————— top of ribbing

——————— outline stitch

:: button

Blooming Tulips Hat

The pattern for this hat was controlled by the yarn I used to create it. First, I wanted to show off the unique thick-and-thin handspun yarn to its best advantage. Second, I knew that I had less wool than I'd usually need to make a hat. To make the yarn stretch, I used larger needles than the ones I'd normally select for a yarn of this weight. However, this choice actually worked to the advantage of the yarn because the thicker parts of handspun yarn were the perfect weight for the needles I was using and this gauge shows off the thick-and-thin yarn well. The downside to this needle choice is that this hat will not be very wind- or waterproof because of the loose gauge.

SIZES
Adult S (M, L)

FINISHED MEASUREMENTS
Circumference: 19½ (21¾, 24)" 50 (55, 61)cm
Height: 7½ (8, 9)" 19 (20, 23)cm

YARN
Approximately 70 (80, 95) yards 64 (73, 87)m
chunky weight 100% wool yarn
Small amount of 100% wool yarn for
embellishment
*Shown: 2-ply thick-and-thin handspun
yarn, thrifted oddments*

NEEDLES
16" (40 cm) US 10½ (6.5mm) circular needle
Set of US 10½ (6.5mm) dpns
*If necessary, change needle size to obtain
correct gauge.*

NOTIONS
Quilting pencil or chalk
Stitch markers
Tapestry needle
3 ½" (13mm) oval buttons

GAUGE
14 sts and 20 rows = 4" (10cm) in St st

KNITTING SKILLS
k2tog [knit 2 together]: Dec by knitting 2 sts
tog as 1 st (see page 22)

EMBELLISHMENT SKILLS
Outline stitch (see page 32)

KNIT
With circular needle, CO 68 (76, 84) sts. Join for working in the rnd,
being careful not to twist sts. Place marker for beg of rnd, if desired.

RND 1: *K2, p2; rep from * to end.

Rep Rnd 1 until work measures 1 (1, 1)" 3 (3, 3)cm.

Change to St st and work until piece measures 5½ (5½, 6)" 14 (14, 15)cm
from cast-on edge.

NEXT RND: *K32 (17, 12), k2tog; rep from * to end—66 (72, 78) sts.

CROWN DECREASES
When knitting on the circular needle becomes uncomfortable, switch
to dpns.

NEXT RND: *K9 (10, 11), k2tog, pm; rep from * to end—60 (66, 72) sts.

Knit 1 rnd.

NEXT RND: *Knit to 2 sts before marker, k2tog; rep from * to end—54
(60, 66) sts.

Rep last 2 rnds 8 (9, 10) times more—6 (6, 6) sts.

Cut yarn, leaving a 6" (15cm) tail. Use tapestry needle to thread tail
through rem sts, pull tight and fasten off. Weave in ends.

EMBELLISH
Transfer the embellishment pattern below to the knitted fabric with
a quilting pencil or chalk. Using wool yarn and a tapestry needle,
stitch the embroidery pattern using outline stitch. Sew on buttons
where indicated.

Pattern | *enlarge template by
150% to bring to full size* ———— top of ribbing

———— outline stitch

button

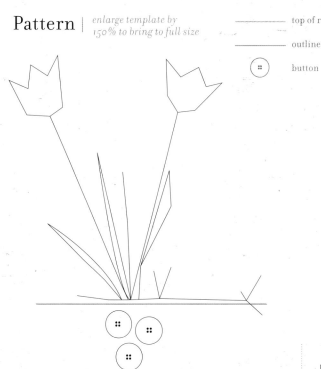

Lollipop Hat

I often try to come up with unusual color combinations on the hats I create for both children and adults. With commercial kids' garments I often find the color palette lacking in pizzazz. The contrasting oranges used in this hat create a cheerful appearance that is more sophisticated than the usual combinations you find on children's garments. Adding to the cheerful nature of this hat, the gentle point at the top looks supercute on the head.

SIZES

Child S (M, L)

FINISHED MEASUREMENTS

Circumference: 16 (17½, 19¼)" 41 (44, 49)cm
Height: 6½ (7, 7¾)" 17 (18, 20)cm

YARN

Approximately 20 (20, 20) yards 18 (18, 18)m
worsted weight 100% wool yarn (A)
Approximately 75 (90, 110) yards 69 (82, 101)m
worsted weight 100% wool yarn (B)
Small amount of 100% wool yarn for
embellishment
Shown: recycled sweater yarn, Cascade 220

NEEDLES

16" (40cm) US 7 (4.5mm) circular needle
Set of US 7 (4.5mm) dpns
*If necessary, change needle size to obtain
correct gauge.*

NOTIONS

Quilting pencil or chalk
Stitch markers
Tapestry needle

GAUGE

20 sts and 28 rows = 4" (10cm) in St st

KNITTING SKILLS

k2tog [knit 2 together]: Dec by knitting 2 sts
tog as 1 st (see page 22)

EMBELLISHMENT SKILLS

Outline stitch (see page 32)

KNIT

With circular needle and yarn A, CO 80 (88, 96) sts. Join for working
in the rnd, being careful not to twist sts. Place marker for beg of rnd,
if desired.

RND 1: *K2, p2; rep from * to end.

Rep Rnd 1 until piece measures 1 (1¼, 1¼)" 3 (3, 3)cm from
cast-on edge.

Change to yarn B and St st and work even until piece measures 4 (4¼,
4½)" 10 (11, 11)cm from cast-on edge.

NEXT RND (S and M only): *K38 (20), k2tog; rep from * to end—78
(84) sts.

CROWN DECREASES

When knitting on the circular needle becomes uncomfortable, switch
to dpns.

NEXT RND: *K11 (12, 14), k2tog, pm; rep from * to end—72 (78, 90) sts.

Knit 1 rnd.

NEXT RND: *Knit to 2 sts before marker, k2tog; rep from * to end—66
(72, 84) sts.

Rep last 2 rnds 10 (11, 13) times more—6 (6, 6) sts.

Cut yarn, leaving a 6" (15cm) tail. Use tapestry needle to thread tail
through rem sts, pull tight and fasten off. Weave in ends.

EMBELLISH

Transfer the embellishment pattern below to the knitted fabric with a
quilting pencil or chalk. Using wool yarn and a tapestry needle, stitch the
embroidery pattern using outline stitch.

Pattern | *enlarge template by 120% for small
(128% medium, 135% large) to bring to full size*

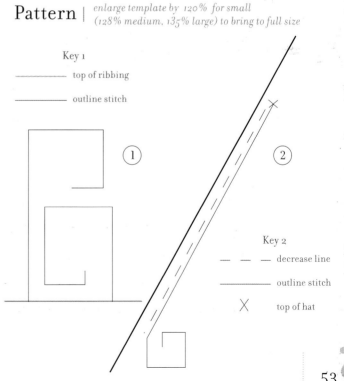

Key 1

------------ top of ribbing

———————— outline stitch

(1)   (2)

Key 2

— — — decrease line

——————— outline stitch

✕   top of hat

Mountain Sunset
Inside Out Hat

I was more than a few rounds into knitting this basic roll-brim hat when I noticed that I liked the inside much more than the outside. So, I ripped back and started anew. The reversed-rolled brim hugs the head nicely and creates a pretty detail that I emphasized with an embellishment at the brim. In addition, this hat is quite warm because it is knitted on needles that are a size smaller than those usually recommended for the weight of the yarn. Using smaller needles creates a thicker fabric that is more wind resistant than yarn knit at the recommended gauge.

sizes

Adult S (M, L)

finished measurements

Circumference: 18 (20½, 22¾)" 46 (52, 58)cm
Height (with brim unrolled): 8½ (9, 9½)" 22
(23, 24)cm

yarn

Approximately 110 (125, 150) yards 101 (114,
137)m worsted weight 100% wool yarn
Small amount of 100% wool yarn for
embellishment
Shown: Noro Silver Thaw, thrifted oddments

needles

16" (40cm) US 6 (4mm) circular needle
Set of US 6 (4mm) dpns
*If necessary, change needle size to obtain
correct gauge.*

notions

Quilting pencil or chalk
Stitch markers
Tapestry needle

gauge

20 sts and 32 rows = 4" (10cm) in reverse St st

knitting skills

k2tog [knit 2 together]: Dec by knitting 2 sts
tog as 1 st (see page 22)

embellishment skills

Outline stitch (see page 32)
Running stitch (see page 32)

KNIT

With circular needle, CO 90 (102, 114) sts. Join for working in the rnd,
being careful not to twist sts. Place marker for beg of rnd, if desired.

Purl 1 rnd.

Change to St st and work even until piece measures 6 (6, 6)" 15 (15, 15)cm
from cast-on edge with the brim unrolled.

CROWN DECREASES

When knitting on the circular needle becomes uncomfortable, switch
to dpns.

NEXT RND: *K13 (15, 17), k2tog, pm; rep from * to end—84 (96, 108) sts.

Knit 1 rnd.

NEXT RND: *Knit to 2 sts before marker, k2tog; rep from * to end—78
(90, 102) sts.

Rep last 2 rnds 12 (14, 16) times more—6 (6, 6) sts.

Cut yarn, leaving a 6" (15cm) tail. Use tapestry needle to thread tail
through rem sts, pull tight and fasten off. Turn hat purl side out.

Weave in ends.

EMBELLISH

Transfer the embellishment pattern below to the knitted fabric with a
quilting pencil or chalk. Using wool yarn and a tapestry needle, stitch
the center of the pattern using outline stitch and stitch the rays using
running stitch.

Pattern | *enlarge template by
120% to bring to full size*

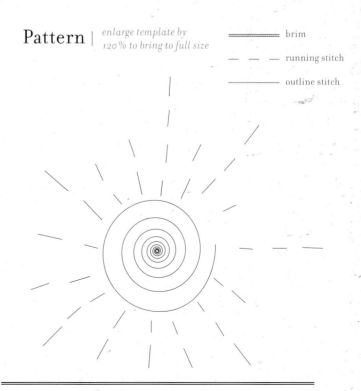

================ brim

— — — running stitch

──────── outline stitch

Berry Bramble Hat

I fell in love with moss stitch when using it on the border of a shawl. Its pebbled texture is a simple and fun accent for any knit. I started the brim of this hat with moss stitch, and then carried the pattern through on the earflaps, which will cover more than just your ears to keep you extra warm. I also added a gently sloping peak at the top to give the hat a more feminine, playful appearance. The pretty buttons and embroidery complete the transformation from a solely utilitarian garment to one that is lovely to look at as well.

SIZES

Adult S (M, L)

FINISHED MEASUREMENTS

Circumference: 20 (21½, 23)" 51 (55, 58)cm
Height: 7½ (8, 8¾)" 19 (20, 22)cm

YARN

Approximately 120 (140, 160) yards 110 (128, 146)m heavy worsted or Aran weight 100% wool yarn

Small amount of 100% wool yarn for embellishment

Shown: 2-ply thick-and-thin handspun yarn, thrifted oddments

NEEDLES

16" (40cm) US 7 (4.5mm) circular needle
Set of US 7 (4.5mm) dpns

If necessary, change needle size to obtain correct gauge.

NOTIONS

Quilting pencil or chalk
Removable markers or safety pins
Stitch markers
Tapestry needle
US G (4.5mm) or H (5mm) crochet hook
5 ½" (13mm) buttons

GAUGE

19 sts and 28 rows = 4" (10cm) in St st

KNITTING SKILLS

k2tog [knit 2 together]: Dec by knitting 2 sts tog as 1 st (see page 22)

est patt [established pattern]: Cont to work in the pattern as it's been established in the previous row/instructions

EMBELLISHMENT SKILLS

Outline stitch (see page 32)
Single satin stitch (see page 32)
Crochet chain edging (see page 34)

KNIT

With circular needle, CO 96 (102, 108) sts. Join for working in the rnd, being careful not to twist sts. Place marker for beg of rnd, if desired.

RNDS 1–2: *K1, p1; rep from * to end.

RNDS 3–4: *P1, k1; rep from * to end.

Rep Rnds 1–4 once more.

Change to St st and work even until piece measures 4 (4, 4½)" 10 (10, 11)cm from cast-on edge.

CROWN DECREASES

When knitting on the circular needle becomes uncomfortable, switch to dpns.

NEXT RND: *K14 (15, 16), k2tog, pm; rep from * to end—90 (96, 102) sts.

Knit 1 rnd.

NEXT RND: *Knit to 2 sts before marker, k2tog; rep from * to end—84 (90, 96) sts.

Rep last 2 rnds 13 (14, 15) times more—6 (6, 6) sts.

Cut yarn, leaving a 6" (15cm) tail. Use tapestry needle to thread tail through rem sts, pull tight and fasten off. Weave in ends.

EARFLAPS

Lay hat flat so that beg of round is at center back. Count 10 (11, 12) sts from center back to the right and mark with safety pin or removable marker (marker 1). Count 22 (22, 22) sts from marker 1 to the right and mark with safety pin or removable marker (marker 2). Count 32 (36, 40) sts from marker 2 to the right and mark with safety pin or removable marker (marker 3). Count 22 (22, 22) sts from marker 3 to the right and mark with safety pin or removable marker (marker 4). With RS facing, pick up and knit 22 (22, 22) sts from cast-on edge, beg at marker 1 and working toward marker 2. (See page 30 for instructions on picking up sts from cast-on edge.)

**Rows 1–2: *K1, p1; rep from * to end.

Rows 3–4 : *P1, k1; rep from * to end.

Next row: Cont in est patt, work to last 3 sts, work 2 tog, work 1—21 (21, 21) sts.

Rep last row 13 times more—8 (8, 8) sts.

Bind off.

For second earflap, pick up and knit 22 (22, 22) sts from cast-on edge, beg at marker 3 and working toward marker 4. Rep from ** to complete second earflap. Weave in ends.

EMBELLISH

Using wool yarn, work a crochet chain edging around the bottom edge of the hat and earflaps. Transfer the embellishment pattern on page 124 to the knitted fabric with a quilting pencil or chalk. Using wool yarn and a tapestry needle, stitch the embroidery pattern using outline stitch and single satin stitch where indicated. Following pattern, sew on buttons.

Pattern | *see page 124*

Pattern | *see page 124*

Lake Reflects Trees Hat

Generally inspired by helmet liners knit for soldiers, I designed this hat to be more of a helmet itself. While other pattern stitches, such as moss stitch and seed stitch, can sometimes give a hat a feminine appearance, garter stitch works well on hats for both men and women, so on this hat I chose to work the brim and earflaps in garter stitch. The dark colors of the yarn were also selected with a man's taste in mind, and for embellishing, I turned to my old standby for men's hats—trees.

sizes

Adult S (M, L)

finished measurements

Circumference: 19½ (21½, 23)" 50 (55, 58)cm
Height: 7½ (8, 8¾)" 19 (20, 22)cm

yarn

Approximately 60 (70, 80) yards 55 (64, 73)m
heavy worsted or Aran weight 100% wool yarn (A)
Approximately 60 (70, 80) yards 55 (64, 73)m
heavy worsted or Aran weight 100% wool yarn (B)
Small amounts of 100% wool yarn in 2 colors for
embellishment
*Shown: Cascade 220, Tahki Donegal Tweed,
thrifted oddments*

needles

16" (40cm) US 8 (5mm) circular needle
Set of US 8 (5mm) dpns
*If necessary, change needle size to obtain
correct gauge.*

notions

Quilting pencil or chalk
Removable markers or safety pins
Stitch markers
Tapestry needle
1 ¾" (2cm) button

gauge

18 sts and 24 rows = 4" (10cm) in St st

knitting skills

k2tog [knit 2 together]: Dec by knitting 2 sts tog
as 1 st (see page 22)

embellishment skills

Outline stitch (see page 32)
Single satin stitch (see page 32)

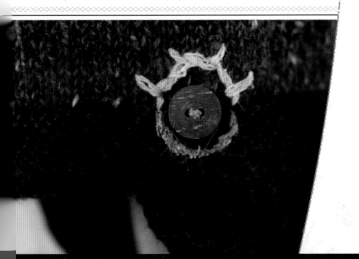

KNIT

With circular needle, CO 88 (96, 104) sts. Join for working in the rnd,
being careful not to twist sts. Place marker for beg of rnd, if desired.

Work even in garter st until piece measures 1½ (1½, 1½)" 4 (4, 4)cm
from cast-on edge.

Change to St st and work even until piece measures 5 (5, 5)" 13 (13,
13)cm from cast-on edge.

CROWN DECREASES

When knitting on the circular needle becomes uncomfortable, switch
to dpns.

NEXT RND: *K9 (10, 11), k2tog, pm; rep from * to end—80 (88, 96) sts.

Knit 1 rnd.

Rep last 2 rnds 9 (10, 11) times more—8 (8, 8) sts.

Cut yarn, leaving a 6" (15cm) tail. Use tapestry needle to thread tail
through rem sts, pull tight and fasten off. Weave in ends.

EARFLAPS

Lay hat flat so that beg of round is at center back. Count 7 (7, 9) sts from
center back to the right and mark with safety pin or removable marker
(marker 1). Count 26 (26, 26) sts from marker 1 to the right and mark
with safety pin or removable marker (marker 2). Count 22 (30, 34) sts
from marker 2 to the right and mark with safety pin or removable marker
(marker 3). Count 26 (26, 26) sts from marker 3 to the right and mark
with safety pin or removable marker (marker 4). With RS facing, pick up
and knit 26 (26, 26) sts from cast-on edge, beg at marker 1 and working
toward marker 2. (See page 30 for instructions on picking up sts from
cast-on edge.)

**Work even in garter st for 4 rows.

NEXT ROW: Knit to last 3 sts, k2tog, k1—25 (25, 25) sts.

Rep last row 12 times more—13 (13, 13) sts.

Bind off.

For second earflap, pick up and knit 26 (26, 26) sts from cast-on edge,
beg at marker 3 and working toward marker 4. Rep from ** to complete
second earflap.

Weave in ends.

EMBELLISH

Transfer the embellishment patterns on page 126 to the knitted fabric
with a quilting pencil or chalk. Using wool yarn and a tapestry needle,
stitch the embroidery pattern using outline stitch and single satin stitch
where indicated. Following pattern, sew on button.

Pattern | *see page 126*

Fresh-Cut Grass Hat

One way to make a warmer hat is to double the fabric. This can be done in a number of ways. My favorite for small hats is a fold-under brim that leaves plenty of space for embroidery. What could be better on a baby hat than lacy edging and a big tassel? When I first dyed the green wool I used to embellish this hat, I knew that I should use it in a way that would show off the depth and diversity of color in it. The tassel and the grass were just the thing.

SIZES

Child S (M, L)

FINISHED Measurements

Circumference: 16¼ (18, 19½)" 41 (46, 50)cm
Height: 5¾ (6½, 7½)" 15 (17, 19) cm

Yarn

Approximately 120 (135, 160) yards 110 (123,
146)m DK or sport weight 100% wool yarn
Small amount of 100% wool yarn for
embellishment
Shown: thrifted oddments

Needles

16" (40cm) US 5 (3.75mm) circular needle
16" (40cm) US 6 (4mm) circular needle
Set of US 6 (4mm) dpns
*If necessary, change needle size to obtain
correct gauge.*

NOTIONS

Stitch markers
Tapestry needle

Gauge

22 sts and 30 rows = 4" (10cm) in St st with
larger needles

Knitting SKILLS

k2tog [knit 2 together]: Dec by knitting 2 sts
tog as 1 st (see page 22)
yo [yarn over]: Wrap the yarn once around the
right-hand needle and cont knitting; on the
subsequent row, treat the wrap as a st, creating
an eyelet hole in the knitted fabric
sl [slip]: Slip st knitwise from left needle to
right needle
psso [pass slipped stitch over]: Insert the left
needle into the sl st on the right needle and pass
it over the st to the left of it and then off of the
right needle (see page 22)

EMBELLISHMENT SKILLS

Outline stitch (see page 32)
Creating decorative tassels (see page 35)

KNIT

With smaller circular needle, CO 90 (99, 108) sts. Join for working in
the rnd, being careful not to twist sts. Place marker for beg of rnd,
if desired.

Work even in St st until piece measures 2 (2, 2¼)" 5 (5, 6)cm from
cast-on edge.

TURNING RND: Knit 0 (1, 0), *k2tog, yo; rep from * around—90
(99, 108) sts.

Change to larger circular needle. Work even in St st until piece measures
4 (4½, 5¼)" 10 (11, 13)cm from turning round.

CROWN DECREASES

When knitting on the circular needle becomes uncomfortable, switch
to dpns.

NEXT RND: *K8 (9, 10), k2tog, pm; rep from * to end—81 (90, 99) sts.

Knit 2 rnds.

NEXT RND: *Knit to 2 sts before marker, k2tog; rep from * to end—72
(81, 90) sts.

Rep last 3 rnds 1 (1, 1) time more—63 (72, 81) sts.

Knit 1 rnd.

NEXT RND: *Knit to 2 sts before marker, k2tog; rep from * to end—54
(63, 72) sts.

Rep last 2 rnds 5 (6, 7) times more—9 (9, 9) sts.

NEXT RND: *Sl 1, k2tog, psso; rep from * around—3 (3, 3) sts.

Cut yarn, leaving a 6" (15cm) tail. Use tapestry needle to thread tail
through rem sts, pull tight and fasten off. Weave in ends.

Fold hem to inside along Turning Rnd. With yarn threaded on tapestry
needle, stitch in place.

EMBELLISH

Using wool yarn and a tapestry needle, stitch blades of grass along the
brim of the hat using outline stitch. Create a tassel from the remaining
embellishment yarn and secure to the top of the hat.

Forest Gnome Hat

I read somewhere that gnomes were known as the keepers of the forest, so I tried to keep this hat mossy, subtle and organic looking while going beyond trees and leaves. The yarn I used to create this hat is called a singles yarn, a yarn made up of one unplied strand. Singles yarns knit up with one side of each stitch longer than the other, creating a fabric that looks like it has straight lines heading up the garment. I emphasized this natural feature of the knitted fabric with the embroidery pattern I chose. I think what made this embroidery successful is the interplay between those lines and the embroidery lines.

sizes

Child S (M, L)

finished measurements

Circumference: 15 (17, 19½)" 38 (43, 50)cm
Height: 10½ (11¼, 12)" 27 (29, 30)cm

yarn

Approximately 100 (120, 135) yards 91 (110, 123)m bulky weight 100% wool yarn (A)
Approximately 15 (15, 15) yards 14 (14, 14)m bulky weight 100% wool yarn (B)
Small amount of 100% wool yarn for embellishment

Shown: recycled sweater yarn, handspun yarn, thrifted oddments

needles

16" (40cm) US 10½ (6.5mm) circular needle
Set of US 10½ (6.5mm) dpns

If necessary, change needle size to obtain correct gauge.

notions

Quilting pencil or chalk
Stitch markers
Tapestry needle

gauge

14 sts and 20 rows = 4" (10cm) in St st

knitting skills

k2tog [knit 2 together]: Dec by knitting 2 sts tog as 1 st (see page 22)

embellishment skills

Outline stitch (see page 32)
Single satin stitch (see page 32)
Creating decorative tassels (see page 35)

KNIT

STRIPE PATTERN

12 rnds yarn A

1 rnd yarn B

Do not cut color not in use, but carry it up the inside of the work.

BRIM

With circular needle and yarn A, CO 52 (60, 68) sts. Join for working in the rnd, being careful not to twist sts. Place marker for beg of rnd, if desired.

Purl 1 rnd.

Change to St st and work even in Stripe Patt until piece measures 4½ (4½, 4½)" 11 (11, 11)cm from cast-on edge.

CROWN DECREASES

When knitting on the circular needle becomes uncomfortable, switch to dpns.

NEXT RND: *K11 (13, 15), k2tog, pm; rep from * to end—48 (56, 64) sts.

Knit 2 rnds.

NEXT RND: *Knit to 2 sts before marker, k2tog; rep from * to end—44 (52, 60) sts.

Rep last 3 rnds 8 (10, 12) times more—12 (12, 12) sts.

Knit 1 rnd.

NEXT RND: *K1, k2tog; rep from * to end—8 (8, 8) sts.

NEXT RND: *K2tog; rep from * to end—4 (4, 4) sts.

Cut yarn, leaving a 6" (15cm) tail. Use tapestry needle to thread tail through rem sts, pull tight and fasten off. Weave in ends.

EMBELLISH

Transfer the embellishment pattern on page 126 to the knitted fabric with a quilting pencil or chalk. Using wool yarn and a tapestry needle, stitch the embroidery pattern using outline stitch and single satin stitch where indicated. Create a tassel from yarn B and secure to the top of the hat.

Pattern | *see page 126*

Apple on the Tree Hat

The recycled sweater wool used in this hat is from a hand-knit sweater. I believe that when I unravel a hand-knit sweater it at least deserves a eulogy. This sweater was beautifully and ingeniously constructed. It took me some serious sweat to get it apart. The wool was perfect for the sweater, and the stitches were even. Unfortunately, the pattern used was dated and bulky, and therefore unlikely to find a good home. I went to the thrift store two or three times before I finally picked it up. Now it lives reincarnated in this hat, and forever in this book.

SIZES
Child S (M, L)

FINISHED MEASUREMENTS
Circumference: 16 (17½, 19¼)" 41 (44, 49)cm
Height (with brim rolled): 6 (6½, 7)" 15
(17, 18)cm

YARN
Approximately 100 (110, 120) yards 91 (101,
110)m worsted weight 100% wool yarn
Small amounts of 100% wool yarn in 4 colors
for embellishment
*Shown: recycled sweater yarn, thrifted
oddments*

NEEDLES
16" (40cm) US 7 (4.5mm) circular needle
Set of US 7 (4.5mm) dpns
*If necessary, change needle size to obtain
correct gauge.*

NOTIONS
Quilting pencil or chalk
Stitch markers
Tapestry needle

GAUGE
19 sts and 28 rows = 4" (10cm) in St st

KNITTING SKILLS
k2tog [knit 2 together]: Dec by knitting 2 sts
tog as 1 st (see page 22)
sl [slip]: Slip st knitwise from left needle to
right needle
SSK [slip, slip, knit]: Dec by slipping 2 sts
knitwise one at a time from left needle to
right needle. Insert the tip of the left needle into the
front of both sts and knit the 2 sts tog as 1 st
(see page 22)
psso [pass slipped stitch over]: Insert the left
needle into the sl st on the right needle and
pass it over the st to the left of it and then off of
the right needle (see page 22)

EMBELLISHMENT SKILLS
Outline stitch (see page 32)

KNIT
With circular needle, CO 76 (84, 92) sts. Join for working in the rnd,
being careful not to twist sts. Place marker for beg of rnd, if desired.

Work even in St st until piece measures 4 (4¼, 4½)" 10 (11, 11)cm from
cast-on edge with brim rolled.

CROWN DECREASES
When knitting on the circular needle becomes uncomfortable, switch
to dpns.

SET-UP RND: *K19 (21, 23), pm; rep from * to end.

NEXT RND: *K2tog, knit to 2 sts before marker, SSK; rep from * to
end—68 (76, 84) sts.

Knit 1 rnd.

Rep last 2 rnds 7 (8, 9) times more—12 (12, 12) sts.

NEXT RND: *Sl 1, k2tog, psso; rep from * to end—4 (4, 4) sts.

Cut yarn, leaving a 6" (15cm) tail. Use tapestry needle to thread tail
through rem sts, pull tight and fasten off. Weave in ends.

EMBELLISH
Transfer the embellishment pattern below to the knitted fabric with a
quilting pencil or chalk. Using wool yarn and a tapestry needle, stitch the
embroidery pattern using outline stitch.

Pattern | *enlarge template by
133% to bring to full size* ═══════ brim
———————— outline stitch
✕ ✕ top of hat

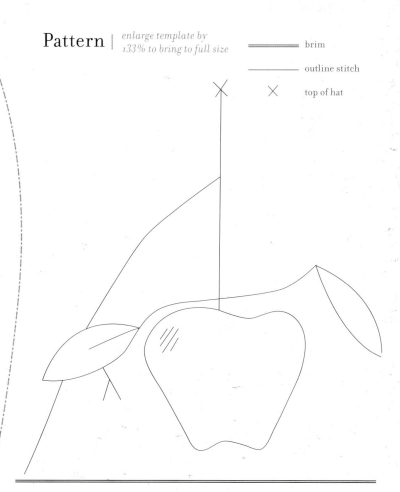

Sweet Pea Hat

This hat turned out a bit shorter than I prefer, but over time I have come to the conclusion that it doesn't always matter what I like, because my friends, family or customers often value something totally different. This short hat may perfectly suit the taste of someone else, or the other elements of the hat may be the attraction for the wearer. The subtle differences in the hand-dyed yarn and the lovely embellishments give this hat a sweet appearance that complements its diminutive size.

sizes

Adult S (M, L)

finished measurements

Circumference (at brim): 15 (17, 19½)" 38 (43, 50)cm

Height: 8 (8½, 9½)" 20 (22, 24)cm

yarn

Approximately 90 (110, 130) yards 82 (101, 119)m worsted weight 100% wool yarn

Small amount of 100% wool yarn for embellishment

Shown: recycled sweater yarn

needles

16" (40cm) US 7 (4.5mm) circular needle

Set of US 7 (4.5mm) dpns

If necessary, change needle size to obtain correct gauge.

notions

Quilting pencil or chalk

Stitch markers

Tapestry needle

1 ¾" (2cm) buttons

3 ½" (13mm) buttons

gauge

21 sts and 29 rows = 4" (10cm) in St st

knitting skills

k2tog [knit 2 together]: Dec by knitting 2 sts tog as 1 st (see page 22)

kfb [knit one front and back]: Inc by knitting into front and back of next st (see page 23)

embellishment skills

Outline stitch (see page 32)

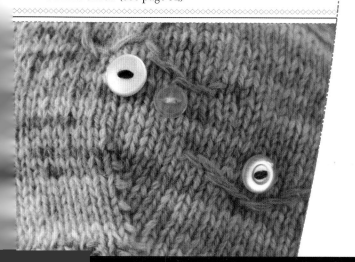

KNIT

With circular needle, CO 78 (90, 102) sts. Join for working in the rnd, being careful not to twist sts. Place marker for beg of rnd, if desired.

RND 1: *K1, p1; rep from * to end.

Rep Rnd 1 once more.

NEXT RND: *K12 (14, 16), kfb, pm; rep from * to end—84 (96, 108) sts.

Knit 1 rnd.

NEXT RND: *Knit to 1 st before marker, kfb; rep from * to end—90 (102, 114) sts.

Rep last 2 rnds 5 times more—120 (132, 144) sts.

Work even in St st until piece measures 3½ (3½, 4)" 9 (9, 10)cm from cast-on edge.

CROWN DECREASES

When knitting on the circular needle becomes uncomfortable, switch to dpns.

NEXT RND: *Knit to 2 sts before marker, k2tog; rep from * to end—114 (126, 138) sts.

Knit 1 rnd.

Rep last 2 rnds 18 (20, 22) times more—6 (6, 6) sts.

Cut yarn, leaving a 6" (15cm) tail. Use tapestry needle to thread tail through rem sts, pull tight and fasten off. Weave in ends.

EMBELLISH

Transfer the embellishment pattern below to the knitted fabric with a quilting pencil or chalk. Using wool yarn and a tapestry needle, stitch the embroidery pattern using outline stitch. Following pattern, sew on buttons.

Pattern | *enlarge template by 167% to bring to full size*

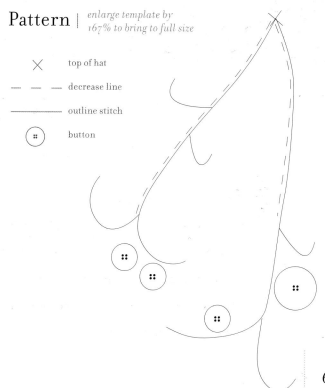

✕   top of hat

— — —   decrease line

————   outline stitch

⊡   button

Root Vegetable Hat

I've done several variations on this hat and it has a finicky character. First, for a proper fit the ribbing needs to be tighter than the body of the hat. I recommend going down a needle size for the ribbing. Second, mohair yarns work up differently than yarns made from other fibers. Mohair with a large halo creates a much larger hat than mohair yarn that is not as fuzzy. The yarn featured in this hat has a large halo, forming a soft, floppy hat. Carefully monitor your gauge as you work on this hat. Measure your hat in progress often and measure it well so that you will not be surprised by your finished project.

SIZES

Adult S (M, L)

FINISHED MEASUREMENTS

Circumference (at brim): 15½ (17, 19½)" 39 (43, 50)cm

Height: 8¼ (9, 9½)" 21 (23, 24)cm

YARN

Approximately 95 (105, 120) yards 87 (96, 110)m chunky weight mohair or mohair blend yarn

Shown: Lang Flair 2000

NEEDLES

16" (40cm) US 8 (5mm) circular needle
16" (40cm) US 9 (5.5mm) circular needle
Set of US 9 (5.5mm) dpns

If necessary, change needle size to obtain correct gauge.

NOTIONS

Stitch markers
Tapestry needle
4 ⅜" (1cm) buttons

GAUGE

16 sts and 22 rows = 4" (10cm) in St st with larger needles

KNITTING SKILLS

k2tog [knit 2 together]: Dec by knitting 2 sts tog as 1 st (see page 22)
kfb [knit one front and back]: Inc by knitting into front and back of next st (see page 23)

KNIT

With smaller circular needle, CO 72 (78, 84) sts. Join for working in the rnd, being careful not to twist sts. Place marker for beg of rnd, if desired.

RND 1: *K1, p1; rep from * to end.

Rep Rnd 1 until piece measures 1 (1, 1)" 3 (3, 3)cm from cast-on edge.

Change to larger circular needle.

NEXT RND: *K11 (12, 13), kfb, pm; rep from * to end—78 (84, 90) sts.

Knit 1 rnd.

NEXT RND: *Knit to 1 st before marker, kfb; rep from * to end—84 (90, 96) sts.

Rep last 2 rnds 3 times more—102 (108, 114) sts.

Work even in St st until piece measures 3½ (4, 4)" 9 (10, 10)cm from cast-on edge.

CROWN DECREASES

When knitting on the circular needle becomes uncomfortable, switch to dpns.

NEXT RND: *Knit to 2 sts before marker, k2tog; rep from * to end—96 (102, 108) sts.

Knit 1 rnd.

Rep last 2 rnds 15 (16, 17) times more—6 (6, 6) sts.

Cut yarn, leaving a 6" (15cm) tail. Use tapestry needle to thread tail through rem sts, pull tight and fasten off. Weave in ends.

EMBELLISH

Sew 4 ⅜" (1cm) buttons onto the brim of the hat.

Back Alley Hat

The inspiration for the embroidery on this hat is from my homeland of Montana. I remember knapweed growing in the alley behind my childhood home. My memories from childhood are full of the purple flowers, which I loved to examine. However, I know now that knapweed is an aggressive weed that is taking over and pushing out many of the native plants. Nonetheless, it is a part of my childhood landscape, and it reminds me of home. For your hat, feel free to choose your own favorite noxious weed to embroider.

SIZES

Adult S (M, L)

FINISHED MEASUREMENTS

Circumference (at brim): 14½ (16¾, 19¼)"
37 (43, 49)cm
Height: 7½ (8, 9)" 19 (20, 23)cm

YARN

Approximately 65 (75, 90) yards 59 (69, 82)m
worsted weight 100% wool yarn (A)
Approximately 65 (75, 90) yards 59 (69, 82)m
worsted weight 100% wool yarn (B)
Small amount of 100% wool yarn for
embellishment
*Shown: Cascade 220, Tahki Donegal Tweed,
thrifted oddments*

NEEDLES

16" (40cm) US 7 (4.5mm) circular needle
Set of US 7 (4.5mm) dpns
*If necessary, change needle size to obtain
correct gauge.*

NOTIONS

Quilting pencil or chalk
Stitch markers
Tapestry needle

GAUGE

20 sts and 30 rows = 4" (10cm) in St st

KNITTING SKILLS

k2tog [knit 2 together]: Dec by knitting 2 sts
tog as 1 st (see page 22)
kfb [knit front and back]: Inc by knitting
into front and back of next st (see page 23)

EMBELLISHMENT SKILLS

Outline stitch (see page 32)

KNIT

STRIPE PATTERN

7 rnds yarn A

7 rnds yarn B

Do not cut color not in use, but carry it up the inside of the work.

*Note: To replicate hat shown, discontinue Stripe Patt after 3 repeats have been
worked and continue with yarn A only.*

BRIM

With circular needle and yarn A, CO 72 (84, 96) sts. Join for working
in the rnd, being careful not to twist sts. Place marker for beg of rnd,
if desired.

RND 1: *K1, p1; rep from * to end.

Rep Rnd 1 once more.

NEXT RND: *K11 (13, 15), kfb, pm; rep from * to end—78 (90, 102) sts.

Knit 1 rnd.

NEXT RND: *Knit to 1 st before marker, kfb; rep from * to end—84
(96, 108) sts.

Rep last 2 rnds 4 times more—108 (120, 132) sts.

Work even in St st until piece measures 4 (4, 4½)" 10 (10, 11)cm from
cast-on edge.

CROWN DECREASES

When knitting on the circular needle becomes uncomfortable, switch
to dpns.

Knit 1 rnd.

NEXT RND: *Knit to 2 sts before marker, k2tog; rep from * to end—102
(114, 126) sts.

Rep last 2 rnds 15 (17, 19) times more—12 (12, 12) sts.

NEXT RND: *K2tog; rep from * to end—6 (6, 6) sts.

Cut yarn, leaving a 6" (15cm) tail. Use tapestry needle to thread tail
through rem sts, pull tight and fasten off. Weave in ends.

EMBELLISH

Transfer the embellishment pattern on page 124 to the knitted fabric
with a quilting pencil or chalk. Using wool yarn and a tapestry needle,
stitch the embroidery pattern using outline stitch.

Pattern | *see page 124*

Snow Princess Hat

For this hat I used a smaller size needle than I normally would because I wanted to create a fabric that was stiff. A stiff fabric holds its shape better and therefore supports the structure of this hat. An additional bonus to working in a different gauge is that the dense fabric is also more wind- and waterproof, so it will easily keep your Snow Princess warm.

SIZES

Child S (M, L)

FINISHED MEASUREMENTS

Circumference (at brim): 14½ (16, 17½)" 37 (41, 44)cm
Height: 6 (6½, 7)" 15 (17, 18)cm

YARN

Approximately 25 (25, 25) yards 23 (23, 23)m worsted weight angora/nylon blend yarn (A)
Approximately 110 (120, 135) yards 101 (110, 123)m worsted weight 100% wool yarn (B)
Shown: recycled sweater yarns

NEEDLES

16" (40cm) US 6 (4mm) circular needle
Set of US 6 (4mm) dpns
If necessary, change needle size to obtain correct gauge.

NOTIONS

Quilting pencil or chalk
Stitch markers
Tapestry needle

GAUGE

20 sts and 28 rows = 4" (10cm) in St st

KNITTING SKILLS

k2tog [knit 2 together]: Dec by knitting 2 sts tog as 1 st (see page 22)
kfb [knit one front and back]: Inc by knitting into front and back of next st (see page 23)

EMBELLISHMENT SKILLS

Outline stitch (see page 32)
Lazy daisy stitch (see page 33)
Creating decorative tassels (see page 35)

KNIT

With circular needle and yarn A, CO 72 (80, 88) sts. Join for working in the rnd, being careful not to twist sts. Place marker for beg of rnd, if desired.

RND 1: *K1, p1; rep from * to end.

Rep Rnd 1 until piece measures ¾ (¾, ¾)" 2 (2, 2)cm.

Change to St st and yarn B and knit 1 rnd.

NEXT RND: *K8 (9, 10), kfb, pm; rep from * to end—80 (88, 96) sts.

Knit 1 rnd.

NEXT RND: *Knit to 1 st before marker, kfb; rep from * to end—88 (96, 104) sts.

Rep last 2 rnds twice more—104 (112, 120) sts.

Work even in St st until piece measures 3¾ (4, 4½)" 10 (10, 11)cm from cast-on edge.

Purl 1 rnd.

Knit 1 rnd.

CROWN DECREASES

When knitting on the circular needle becomes uncomfortable, switch to dpns.

NEXT RND: *Knit to 2 sts before marker, k2tog; rep from * to end—96 (104, 112) sts.

Knit 1 rnd.

Rep last 2 rnds 5 (6, 6) times more—56 (56, 64) sts.

NEXT RND: *Knit to 2 sts before marker, k2tog; rep from * to end—48 (48, 56) sts.

Rep last rnd 5 (5, 6) times more—8 (8, 8) sts.

Cut yarn, leaving a 6" (15cm) tail. Use tapestry needle to thread tail through rem sts, pull tight and fasten off. Weave in ends.

EMBELLISH

Transfer the embellishment pattern below to the knitted fabric with a quilting pencil or chalk. Using yarn A and a tapestry needle, stitch the embroidery pattern using outline stitch and lazy daisy stitch. Create a tassel from yarn A and secure to the top of the hat.

Pattern | *enlarge template by 133% to bring to full size*

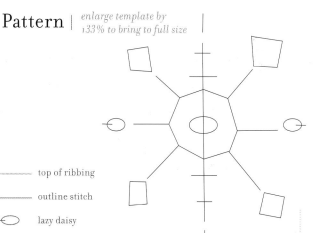

———————— top of ribbing

———————— outline stitch

lazy daisy

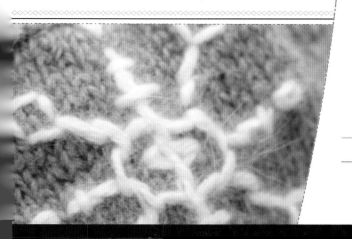

Headgear

Some of the hats in this chapter march to the beat of a different drummer—and some of them aren't really hats at all! The projects in this chapter fall into three different categories: flat hats, bonnets and headbands.

I have a fervent love of flat hats, especially because they provide a fine surface to embroider on. Perhaps it is because they remind me of a canvas, with the added bonus that I can embellish the back as well as the front. Plus, who knew that a square, sewn across the top into a pocket shape, would fit so nicely and look so cute on everyone from an adult to a baby? The only tricky part of knitting these flat hats is that you have to learn two new bind-off methods, which you can find on pages 27–29. Square hats, such as the *All Things Grow Hat* on page 76, use the three-needle bind off. Angled hats, like the *Biker Hat* on page 82, use Kitchener stitch. Don't be afraid of these—they're useful techniques to know and once you get them down, you'll have them for life.

Bonnets are a fun new shape that I have been experimenting with recently. Knit flat, they are ingeniously folded or seamed to create a hoodlike hat. Because they are worn so close to the head, they will keep you warm and toasty. As an added bonus, they also provide a large surface for embellishment, which the *Butterfly Pixie Bonnet* on page 90 takes full advantage of.

Headbands are a great transitional piece of clothing. In the spring and autumn when you may just need a little bit of warmth (and style!), they're perfect. They're very quick to knit, so you can easily have one for each piece of your wardrobe. And, you can make headbands that are adjustable to fit any head, like the *Fruit Punch Headband* on page 96. I must confess that I am not a headband wearer. I started knitting them because I have friends and family who refuse to wear hats. I, who so dearly loves making hats, cannot, no matter how much I want to, force my family and friends to do my bidding. So, I compromised.

All Things Grow Hat

This little hat is as cute as can be and as easy as pie. It is the perfect beginner hat. No decreasing and no shaping, but still a great final product. One of my major inspirations for embroidery is food and the natural world that produces it. All of the hats that I embroider with food images are hats of prayer, wonder and thanks. I also like to think of them as educational—this one shows that beets grow in the ground and are fed by the sun. This makes for a hat that is perfect for small children or for foodies and nature lovers.

SIZES

Child S (M, L)

FINISHED MEASUREMENTS

Circumference: 15¼ (16¾, 18½)" 39 (43, 47)cm

Height (with brim rolled): 6 (6½, 7)" 15 (17, 18)cm

YARN

Approximately 100 (110, 130) yards 91 (101, 119)m worsted weight 100% wool yarn in 3 colors

Small amounts of 100% wool yarn in 4 colors for embellishment

Shown: handspun yarn by Daniela Kloppman FeltStudio, recycled sweater yarn, thrifted oddments

NEEDLES

16" (40cm) US 7 (4.5mm) circular needle

Set of US 7 (4.5mm) straight needles

If necessary, change needle size to obtain correct gauge.

NOTIONS

Quilting pencil or chalk

Stitch markers

Tapestry needle

GAUGE

20 sts and 30 rows = 4" (10cm) in St st

KNITTING SKILLS

three-needle bind off: form a seam between two pieces of fabric by knitting one st from each side tog as 1 st (see page 27)

EMBELLISHMENT SKILLS

Outline stitch (see page 32)

KNIT

With circular needle, CO 76 (84, 92) sts. Join for working in the rnd, being careful not to twist sts. Place marker for beg of rnd, if desired.

Work even in St st until piece measures 6 (6½, 7)" 15 (17, 18)cm from cast-on edge with brim rolled.

Transfer sts evenly to two straight needles. Use the circular needle to join top with a three-needle bind off.

Weave in ends.

EMBELLISH

Transfer the embellishment pattern below to the knitted fabric with a quilting pencil or chalk. Using wool yarn and a tapestry needle, stitch the embroidery pattern using outline stitch.

Pattern | *enlarge template by 167% to bring to full size*

- - - - - - edge of knitting

——————— outline stitch

X top of hat

Nautical Nellie Hat

As I was knitting it, this hat reminded me of a poster from World War I that hangs in my bedroom. It shows a woman wearing a sailor uniform with the caption, "Gee!! I wish I were a man. I'd join the Navy." This hat is named after both that poster and my Great-Grandmother Nellie, who lived during that era.

This hat combines three different weights of yarn to make an interesting fabric. The reason the yarns all work well together is that I made this hat to fit loosely, so the changes don't disrupt the fabric much. As you may imagine, this hat varies in how windproof it is accordingly with each stripe. Consider trying fun and fancy yarns like mohair mixed in with your standard yarns for more variety.

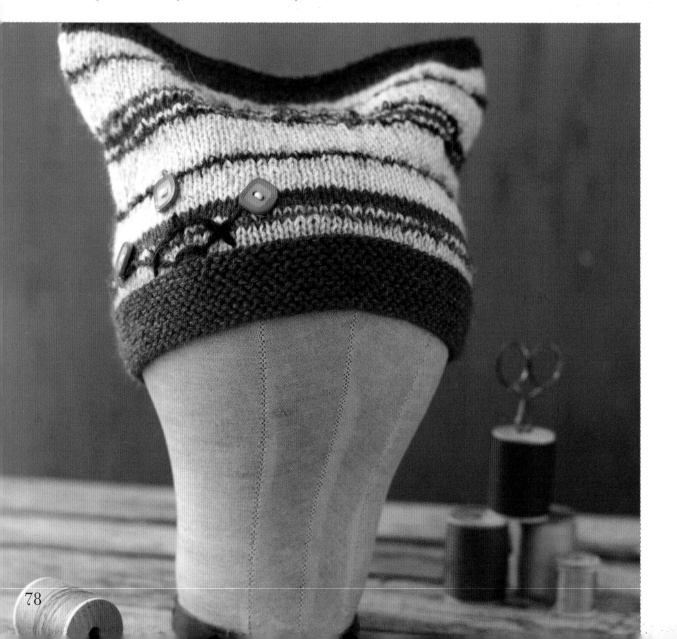

sizes

Adult S (M, L)

finished measurements

Circumference: 18 (20, 22)" 46 (51, 56)cm
Height: 8 (8, 8½)" 20 (20, 22)cm

yarn

Approximately 50 (55, 65) yards 46 (50, 59)m
worsted weight 100% wool yarn (A)
Approximately 60 (70, 80) yards 55 (64, 73)m
worsted weight 100% wool yarn (B)
Approximately 10 (10, 10) yards 9 (9, 9)m
worsted weight 100% wool yarn (C)
Small amount of 100% wool yarn for
embellishment

*Shown: Cascade 220, recycled sweater yarn,
thrifted oddments*

needles

16" (40cm) US 7 (4.5mm) circular needle
Set of US 7 (4.5mm) straight needles

*If necessary, change needle size to obtain
correct gauge.*

notions

Quilting pencil or chalk
Stitch markers
Tapestry needle
3 ⅝" (16mm) buttons

gauge

20 sts and 28 rows = 4" (10cm) in St st

knitting skills

three-needle bind off: form a seam between
two pieces of fabric by knitting one st from
each side tog as 1 st (see page 27)

embellishment skills

Outline stitch (see page 32)

KNIT

STRIPE PATTERN

After brim, knit hat using yarn B with rows of yarn A and yarn C added at
random intervals.

Do not cut color not in use, but carry it up the side of the work.

BRIM

With circular needle and yarn A, CO 90 (100, 110) sts. Join for working
in the rnd, being careful not to twist sts. Place marker for beg of rnd,
if desired.

Work in garter st until piece measures 1½ (1½, 1½)" 4 (4, 4)cm from
cast-on edge.

Change to St st and Stripe Patt and work even until piece measures 7¼
(7¼, 7¾)" 18 (18, 20)cm from cast-on edge.

Change to yarn A and work even until piece measures 8 (8, 8¼)" 20 (20,
21)cm from cast-on edge.

Transfer sts evenly to two straight needles. Use the circular needle to
join top with a three-needle bind off.

Weave in ends.

EMBELLISH

Transfer the embellishment pattern below to the knitted fabric with
a quilting pencil or chalk. Using wool yarn and a tapestry needle,
stitch the embroidery pattern using outline stitch. Sew on buttons
where indicated.

Pattern | *Template shown
at actual size*

— — — — top of garter stitch

——— outline stitch

⬚ button

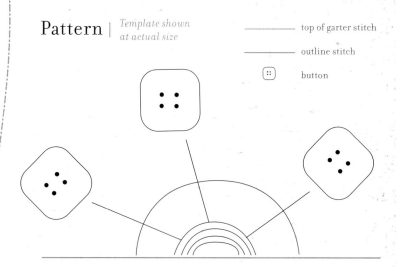

1970s Ski Sweater Hat

This hat is based on a commercial 1970s wool ski sweater that I found at a garage sale in my hometown. I owned and wore many such sweaters in high school. The main yarn in this hat is handspun, hand-dyed wool from Daniela Kloppman FeltStudio. I enjoy knitting with this company's handspun yarns because they always come out beautiful, but slightly different than I expect. Each stitch is a treat.

SIZES
Adult S (M, L)

FINISHED MEASUREMENTS
Circumference: 19½ (21¼, 23)" 50 (54, 58)cm
Height: 7½ (8, 9)" 19 (20, 23)cm

YARN
Approximately 20 (20, 30) yards 18 (18, 27)m
heavy worsted or Aran weight 100% wool
yarn (A)
Approximately 100 (110, 130) yards 91 (101,
119)m heavy worsted or Aran weight 100%
wool yarn (B)
Small amounts of 100% wool yarn in 3 colors
for embellishment
*Shown: handspun yarn by Daniela
Kloppman FeltStudio, recycled sweater yarn*

NEEDLES
16" (40cm) US 8 (5mm) circular needle
Set of US 8 (5mm) dpns
*If necessary, change needle size to obtain
correct gauge.*

NOTIONS
Stitch markers
Tapestry needle

GAUGE
18 sts and 26 rows = 4" (10cm) in St st

KNITTING SKILLS
k2tog [knit 2 together]: Dec by knitting 2 sts
tog as 1 st (see page 22)
SSK [slip, slip, knit]: Dec by slipping 2 sts
knitwise one at a time from left needle to right
needle. Insert the tip of the left needle into
the front of both sts and knit the 2 sts tog as 1
st (see page 22)

EMBELLISHMENT SKILLS
Outline stitch (see page 32)

KNIT
With circular needle and yarn A, CO 88 (96, 104) sts. Join for working
in the rnd, being careful not to twist sts. Place marker for beg of rnd,
if desired.

RND 1: *K2, p2; rep from * to end.

Rep Rnd 1 until piece measures 1¼ (1¼, 1¼)" 3 (3, 3)cm from
cast-on edge.

Change to yarn B and St st and work even until piece measures 4½
(5, 6)" 11 (13, 15)cm from cast-on edge.

CROWN DECREASES
When knitting on the circular needle becomes uncomfortable, switch
to dpns.

SET-UP RND: *K44 (48, 52), pm; rep from * to end.

NEXT RND: *K1, k2tog, knit to 3 sts before marker, SSK, k1; rep from *
to end—84 (92, 100) sts.

Knit 1 rnd.

Rep last 2 rnds 11 times more—40 (48, 56) sts.

Arrange sts on dpns so that first 20 (24, 28) sts of rnd are on one
needle, and rem 20 (24, 28) sts are on a second needle. Graft sts
together with Kitchener st. (See pages 28-29 for instructions on
seaming with Kitchener st.)

Weave in ends.

EMBELLISH
Using contrasting colors of wool yarn and a tapestry needle, stitch three
curved lines on the front of the hat using outline stitch.

Biker Hat

When I was writing this pattern, I was trying to create a hat in a child's large size. You can imagine how surprised I was when I put it on my head and it fit! Creating a stretchy fabric makes for a very forgiving hat, at least in terms of size. I was a wee bit skeptical of the colors I chose for this hat. It wasn't until I imagined it with light yellow embroidery that I knew that the color scheme would work. The shaping of this hat is very similar to the *1970s Ski Sweater Hat* on page 80, but the beginning of the round is located in the back so that the jog in the stripes is at the back of the head rather than the side. Small details like this make a big difference in the finished appearance of a hat. For embellishment, feel free to substitute your own message, such as RECYCLE, EAT or RUN.

SIZES
Adult S (M, L)

FINISHED MEASUREMENTS
Circumference: 18½ (20, 21½)" 47 (51, 55)cm
Height: 7 (7¾, 8½)" 18 (20, 22)cm

YARN
Approximately 35 (40, 50) yards 32 (37, 46)m
worsted weight 100% wool yarn (A)
Approximately 35 (40, 50) yards 32 (37, 46)m
worsted weight 100% wool yarn (B)
Approximately 35 (40, 50) yards 32 (37, 46)m
worsted weight 100% wool yarn (C)
Small amount of 100% wool yarn for
embellishment
Shown: thrifted oddments

NEEDLES
16" (40cm) US 7 (4.5mm) circular needle
Set of US 7 (4.5mm) dpns
*If necessary, change needle size to obtain
correct gauge.*

NOTIONS
Quilting pencil or chalk
Stitch markers
Tapestry needle

GAUGE
20 sts and 26 rows = 4" (10cm) in St st

KNITTING SKILLS
k2tog [knit 2 together]: Dec by knitting 2 sts
tog as 1 st (see page 22)
SSK [slip, slip, knit]: Dec by slipping 2 sts
knitwise one at a time from left needle to
right needle. Insert the tip of the left needle
into the front of both sts and knit the 2 sts tog
as 1 st (see page 22)

EMBELLISHMENT SKILLS
Outline stitch (see page 32)

KNIT

STRIPE PATTERN
3 rnds yarn A

3 rnds yarn B

3 rnds yarn C

Do not cut color not in use, but carry it up the inside of the work.

BRIM
With circular needle and yarn C, CO 92 (100, 108) sts. Join for working
in the rnd, being careful not to twist sts. Place marker for beg of rnd,
if desired.

RND 1: *K2, p2; rep from * to end.

RND 2: K1, *p2, k2; rep from * to last 3 sts, p2, k1.

Rep Rnds 1-2 until piece measures 1 (1, 1)" 3 (3, 3)cm from cast-on edge.

Change to St st and Stripe Patt and work even until piece measures 4
(4¾, 5½)" 10 (12, 14)cm from cast-on edge.

CROWN DECREASES
When knitting on the circular needle becomes uncomfortable, switch
to dpns.

SET-UP RND: K23 (25, 27), pm, k46 (50, 54), pm, k23 (25, 27).

NEXT RND: *Knit to 3 sts before marker, SSK, k1, sm, k1, k2tog; rep
from * once more, knit to end—88 (96, 104) sts.

Knit 1 rnd.

Rep last 2 rnds 11 times more—44 (52, 60) sts.

Arrange sts on dpns so that the 22 (26, 30) sts between the first and
second marker are on one needle and the rem 22 (26, 30) sts are on a
second needle. Graft sts together with Kitchener st. (See pages 28-29 for
instructions on seaming with Kitchener st.)

Weave in ends.

EMBELLISH
Transfer the embellishment pattern below to the knitted fabric with a
quilting pencil or chalk. Using wool yarn and a tapestry needle, stitch the
embroidery pattern using outline stitch.

Pattern | *enlarge template by
133% to bring to full size*
———— top of ribbing
———— outline stitch

Daisy Helmet Hat

This has quickly become one of my favorite baby hat patterns because not only is it dang cute, but the earflaps nearly push it over the edge to adorable. If you choose to embellish children's hats with buttons, my friend Susan, and the Federal regulations for toys, recommend that buttons be used only on hats for children three years old and up. When I put buttons on my smaller hats, I recommend parental supervision while they are being worn. Please do not let your children eat the buttons on their hats. Mostly, I try not to tempt myself by looking in my button tins when making baby hats, but sometimes I can't resist.

SIZES
Child S (M, L)

FINISHED Measurements
Circumference: 16 (17½, 19)" 41 (44, 48)cm
Height: 5 (5½, 6)" 13 (14, 15)cm

YARN
Approximately 30 (35, 40) yards 27 (32, 37)m
worsted weight 100% wool yarn (A)
Approximately 35 (40, 45) yards 32 (37, 41)m
worsted weight 100% wool yarn (B)
Approximately 35 (40, 45) yards 32 (37, 41)m
worsted weight 100% wool yarn (C)
Small amount of 100% wool yarn for
embellishment
Shown: thrifted oddments

NEEDLES
16" (40cm) US 7 (4.5mm) circular needle
Set of US 7 (4.5mm) straight needles
*If necessary, change needle size to obtain
correct gauge.*

NOTIONS
Quilting pencil or chalk
Removable markers or safety pins
Stitch markers
Tapestry needle
1 ⅝" (2cm) button

GAUGE
20 sts and 28 rows = 4" (10cm) in St st

KNITTING SKILLS
three-needle bind off: form a seam between
two pieces of fabric by knitting one st from
each side tog as 1 st (see page 27)
est patt [established pattern]: Cont to work
in the pattern as it's been established in the
previous row/instructions
k2tog [knit 2 together]: Dec by knitting 2 sts
tog as 1 st (see page 22)
SSK [slip, slip, knit]: Dec by slipping 2 sts
knitwise one at a time from left needle to
right needle. Insert the tip of the left needle
into the front of both sts and knit the 2 sts tog
as 1 st (see page 22)
work 2 tog [work 2 together]: Dec by k2tog or
SSK, following est patt

EMBELLISHMENT SKILLS
Lazy daisy stitch (see page 33)

KNIT

BOX STITCH
RNDS 1–2: *K2, p2; rep from * to end.

RNDS 3–4: *P2, k2; rep from * to end.

BRIM
With circular needle and yarn A, CO 80 (88, 96) sts. Join for working
in the rnd, being careful not to twist sts. Place marker for beg of rnd,
if desired.

Work in Box St for 8 rnds. Change to yarn B and St st and work even until
piece measures 3 (3½, 4)" 8 (9, 10)cm from cast-on edge.

Change to yarn C and work even in St st until piece measures 5 (5½, 6)"
13 (14, 15)cm from cast-on edge.

Transfer sts evenly to two straight needles. Use the circular needle to
join top with a three-needle bind off.

Weave in ends.

EARFLAPS
Lay hat flat so that beg of round is at center back. Count 10 (10, 10) sts
from center back to the right and mark with safety pin or removable
marker (marker 1). Count 20 (24, 28) sts from marker 1 to the right and
mark with safety pin or removable marker (marker 2). Count 20 (20, 20)
sts from marker 2 to the right and mark with safety pin or removable
marker (marker 3). Count 20 (24, 28) sts from marker 3 to the right and
mark with safety pin or removable marker (marker 4). With RS facing,
pick up and knit 20 (24, 28) sts from cast-on edge, beg at marker 1 and
working toward marker 2. (See page 30 for instructions on picking up sts
from cast-on edge.)

**Work in Box Stitch for 2 rows.

NEXT ROW: Continue in est patt, work to last 3 sts, work 2 tog, work
1—19 (23, 27) sts.

Rep last row 13 (15, 17) times more—6 (8, 10) sts.

BO.

For second earflap, pick up and knit 20 (24, 28) sts from cast-on edge,
beg at marker 3 and working toward marker 4. Rep from ** to complete
second earflap. Weave in ends.

EMBELLISH
Transfer the embellishment pattern on page 125 to the knitted fabric
with a quilting pencil or chalk. Using wool yarn and a tapestry needle,
stitch the embroidery pattern using lazy daisy stitch. Following pattern,
sew on a button.

Pattern | *see page 125*

Yellow Bells Jester Hat

I could not resist the little ball of handspun yarn I used in this hat because it matched so many of the flowers that were blooming when I was writing this book! Inspiration like this is the reason why I think everyone should have a little basket of yarns just lying around. The jester top on this hat is a fun take on the flat hat that is easy to do. It's a great last-minute technique to spruce up a hat, or sometimes, to save a hat that's not working out well.

SIZES

Child S (M, L)

FINISHED MEASUREMENTS

Circumference: 16 (17¼, 18½)" 41
(44, 47)cm
Height: 5½ (6¼, 7¼)" 14 (16, 18)cm

YARN

Approximately 15 (15, 15) yards 14 (14, 14)m
heavy worsted or Aran weight 100% wool
yarn (A)
Approximately 50 (70, 70) yards 46 (64,64)m
heavy worsted or Aran weight 100% wool
yarn (B)
*Shown: handspun yarn by Daniela
Kloppman FeltStudio, recycled sweater yarn*

NEEDLES

16" (40cm) US 8 (5mm) circular needle
Set of US 8 (5mm) dpns
*If necessary, change needle size to obtain
correct gauge.*

NOTIONS

Quilting pencil or chalk
Stitch markers
Tapestry needle

GAUGE

18 sts and 28 rows = 4" (10cm) in St st

KNITTING SKILLS

three-needle bind off: form a seam between
two pieces of fabric by knitting one st from
each side tog as 1 st (see page 27)

EMBELLISHMENT SKILLS

Outline stitch (see page 32)

KNIT

With circular needle and yarn A, CO 72 (78, 84) sts. Join for working
in the rnd, being careful not to twist sts. Place marker for beg of rnd,
if desired.

Knit 4 rnds.

NEXT RND: *K1, p1; rep from * to end.

Rep last rnd once more.

Change to yarn B and St st and work even until piece measures 4¼
(5, 6)" 11 (13, 15)cm from cast-on edge.

Change to yarn A and work even in St st until piece measures 5½
(6¼, 7¼)" 14 (16, 18)cm from cast-on edge.

*Place next 12 (13, 14) sts of rnd onto one dpn. Place following 12
(13, 14) sts onto a second dpn. Use a third needle to join the sts on
these two needles with a three-needle bind off.

Rep from * twice more.

Use yarn tail to close hole at top of hat. Weave in ends.

EMBELLISH

Transfer the embellishment pattern below to the knitted fabric
with a quilting pencil or chalk. Using wool yarn and a tapestry needle,
stitch the embroidery pattern using outline stitch.

Pattern | *Template shown
at actual size*

.... begin/end
yarn B

——————— outline stitch

end yarn B

begin yarn B

Twirly Girl Bonnet

When I first saw this wonderful handspun yarn, I couldn't resist its beauty and subtlety and I cast on with it right away. For added warmth, I made this bonnet using garter stitch, which is a natural insulator because it makes a thicker fabric than stockinette. Even though this bonnet does not fully cover your head, it will keep you warm! One important feature is the stretchiness of the finished fabric. To make a stretchy fabric, use the largest size knitting needle recommended for the yarn you choose.

SIZES

Adult S (M, L)

FINISHED MEASUREMENTS

7 (8½, 10)" 18 (22, 25)cm square

YARN

Approximately 120 (170, 220) yards 110 (155, 201)m heavy worsted or Aran weight wool blend yarn
Small amount of 100% wool yarn for embellishment
Shown: handspun yarn by Feral Feminine, thrifted oddments

NEEDLES

Set of US 10 (6mm) straight needles
If necessary, change needle size to obtain correct gauge.

NOTIONS

Quilting pencil or chalk
Tapestry needle
1 1" (3cm) button

GAUGE

16 sts and 32 rows = 4" (10cm) in garter st

EMBELLISHMENT SKILLS

Outline stitch (see page 32)

KNIT

CO 28 (34, 40) sts.

Work in garter st until piece measures 14½ (17½, 20½)" 37 (44, 52) cm from cast-on edge.

BO.

Weave in ends.

Lay knitted rectangle flat with the long edge of the rectangle horizontal. Fold the top two corners of the rectangle in toward the center of the bottom edge until they overlap slightly (see diagram below). Using wool yarn and a tapestry needle, tack the top two corners together.

EMBELLISH

Transfer the embellishment pattern below to the knitted fabric with a quilting pencil or chalk. Using wool yarn and a tapestry needle, stitch the embroidery pattern using outline stitch. Sew a button over the corners that have been tacked together. Attach six strands of yarn to each untacked corner and braid them, forming ties for the bonnet.

Assembly

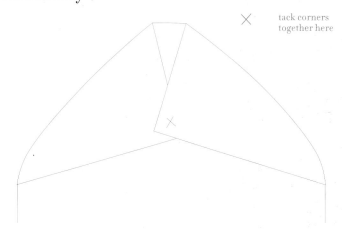

tack corners together here

Pattern | *enlarge template by 200% to bring to full size*

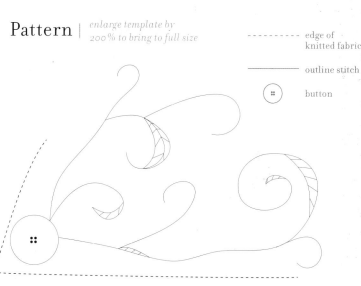

– – – – – – edge of knitted fabric

——— outline stitch

⊞ button

Butterfly Pixie Bonnet

After I made the *Twirly Girl Bonnet* on page 88, all I wanted to do was experiment with other bonnet shapes. I created this bonnet the very next day. Originally, I put this handspun yarn up for sale in my shop. But, after seeing it on top of a pile of yarns for a few days, I couldn't resist it any longer. It hadn't sold, so I took it out of the shop and used it for my own. I'm glad I did, because the thick yarn made a warm, cozy bonnet. If you are making this bonnet for a child younger than three, I recommend using Velcro to fasten the chin strap instead of a button.

SIZES

Child S (M, L)

FINISHED MEASUREMENTS

Circumference: 13 (15, 17)" 33 (38, 43)cm
Height: 5¾ (6¼, 7)" 15 (16, 18)cm

YARN

Approximately 65 (70, 85) yards 59 (64, 78)m
bulky weight 100% wool yarn
Small amount of 100% wool yarn for
embellishment

*Shown: 2-ply thick-and-thin handspun
yarn, thrifted oddments*

NEEDLES

Set of US 10½ (6.5mm) straight needles

*If necessary, change needle size to obtain
correct gauge.*

NOTIONS

Quilting pencil or chalk
Tapestry needle
1 ½" (1cm) button

GAUGE

14 sts and 21 rows = 4" (10cm) in St st

KNITTING SKILLS

yo [yarn over]: Wrap the yarn once around
the right-hand needle and cont knitting; on
the subsequent row, treat the wrap as a st,
creating an eyelet hole in the knitted fabric
p2tog [purl 2 together]: Dec by purling 2 sts
tog as 1 st
k2tog [knit 2 together]: Dec by knitting 2 sts
tog as 1 st (see page 22)

EMBELLISHMENT SKILLS

Running stitch (see page 32)
Single satin stitch (see page 32)

KNIT

CO 60 (68, 76) sts.

Knit 3 rows.

BUTTONHOLE ROW (WS): K2, yo, p2tog, purl to last 2 sts, k2—60
(68, 76) sts.

Knit 1 row.

NEXT ROW (WS): K2, purl to last 2 sts, k2.

NEXT ROW (RS): K2, k2tog, knit to last 4 sts, k2tog, k2—58 (66, 74) sts.

Rep last 2 rows 6 (7, 8) times more—46 (52, 58) sts.

Work even in St st, keeping 2 sts at each end in garter st, until piece
measures 5¾ (6¼, 6¾)" 15 (16, 17)cm from cast-on edge, ending with a
WS row.

Divide sts evenly over 2 needles—23 (26, 29) sts each needle. Graft sts
together with Kitchener st. (See pages 28-29 for instructions on seaming
with Kitchener st.)

Weave in ends.

EMBELLISH

Transfer the embellishment pattern on page 125 to the knitted fabric
with a quilting pencil or chalk. Using wool yarn and a tapestry needle,
stitch the embroidery pattern using running stitch and single satin stitch
where indicated. Sew a button opposite the buttonhole.

Pattern | *see page 125*

Daffodil Headband

Most headbands have to be made to fit snugly on the head in order to stay on, but I made this headband with ties so that it is adjustable to fit the wearer. The knitted portion is long enough to cover the ears for warmth, but short enough to leave room for adjustment in the back. The length of the stockinette section of knitting between the increase and decrease sections can also be adjusted for a customized fit. To embellish this headband, I used some wonderful scraps of handmade wool felt. I enjoyed finding a use for these beautiful bits that other craftspeople could no longer use.

sizes

Child M-L/Adult S (Adult M-L)

finished measurements

Length (not including ties): 17 (21)" 43 (53)cm
Width (at widest point): 3¾ (4¾)" 10 (12)cm

yarn

Approximately 70 (85) yards 64 (78)m DK or
sport weight 100% wool yarn

Small amount of 100% wool yarn for
embellishment

Shown: recycled sweater yarn, thrifted oddments

needles

US 6 (4mm) straight needles
two US 6 (4mm) dpns for i-cord
*If necessary, change needle size to obtain
correct gauge.*

notions

Quilting pencil or chalk
Stitch markers
Tapestry needle
Wool felt scraps
*Shown: felt scraps from Scatterbox Originals and
Mwah! Creations*

gauge

24 sts and 34 rows = 4" (10cm) in St st

knitting skills

M1L [make 1 left]: Inc by knitting into the bar
between sts to create a new st that leans to the
left (see page 24)
M1R [make 1 right]: Inc by knitting into the
bar between sts to create a new st that leans to
the right (see page 25)
k2tog [knit 2 together]: Dec by knitting 2 sts
tog as 1 st (see page 22)
SSK (slip, slip, knit): Dec by slipping 2 sts
knitwise one at a time from left needle to right
needle. Insert the tip of the left needle into the
front of both sts and knit the 2 sts tog as 1 st
(see page 22)

embellishment skills

Outline stitch (see page 32)

KNIT

CO 3 (3) sts.

INCREASE SECTION

ROW 1 (RS): K1, M1L, pm, k1, pm, M1R, k1—5 (5) sts.

ROW 2 (WS): K2, purl to last 2 sts, k2.

ROW 3: Knit to marker, M1L, sm, k1, sm, M1R, knit to end—7 sts.

ROW 4: Rep Row 2.

ROW 5: Knit.

Rep Rows 2–5 8 (11) times more—23 (29) sts.

Work even in St st, keeping 2 sts at each edge in garter st, until piece
measures 12½ (15½)" 32 (39)cm, ending with a WS row.

DECREASE SECTION

ROW 1 (RS): Knit to 2 sts before marker, SSK, sm, k1, sm, k2tog, knit to
end—21 (27) sts.

ROW 2 (WS): K2, purl to last 2 sts, k2.

ROW 3: Knit.

ROW 4: K2, purl to last 2 sts, k2.

Rep Rows 1–4 7 (10) times more—7 (7) sts.

NEXT ROW (RS): K1, SSK, k1, k2tog, k1—5 (5) sts.

NEXT ROW (WS): K2, p1, k2.

NEXT ROW (RS): SSK, k1, k2tog—3 (3) sts.

BO.

TIES

With a dpn, pick up and knit 3 sts from cast-on edge. (See page 30 for
instructions on picking up sts from cast-on edge.) Work I-cord over
these sts for 9½ (11½)" 24 (29)cm. (See page 31 for instructions on
knitting I-cord.) Bind off. Repeat on bound-off edge of headband for
second tie.

Weave in ends. Block.

EMBELLISH

Transfer the embellishment pattern below to the knitted fabric with a
quilting pencil or chalk. Using wool yarn and a tapestry needle, stitch
the embroidery pattern using outline stitch. Trim and attach wool felt
scraps as shown.

Pattern | *enlarge template by 200% to bring to full size*

——————— outline stitch

felt

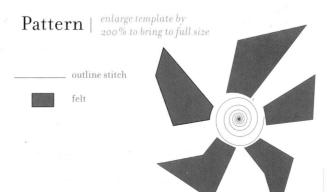

Flapper Eyelet Headband

This pattern originated when I wanted to start making headbands for my friends and family who wouldn't wear hats. I had great difficulty with flashbacks to the early 1990s ski hills, but found a good compromise when I added fringe and embellishments to one side like those found on flappers' headwear. I thoroughly enjoy trying to design new creative embellishments for each one. The simple lace pattern on this headband adds a delicate and lovely touch, even though it is made from worsted weight wool.

SIZES
Adult S (M, L)

FINISHED MEASUREMENTS
Circumference: 16 (17½, 19¼)" 41 (44, 49)cm
Width (unrolled): 3¼ (3¼, 3¼)" 8 (8, 8)cm

YARN
Approximately 65 (75, 75) yards 59 (69, 69)m
worsted weight 100% wool yarn
Small amount of 100% wool yarn for
embellishment
Shown: Cascade 220, thrifted oddments

NEEDLES
16" (40cm) US 7 (4.5mm) circular needle
*If necessary, change needle size to obtain
correct gauge.*

NOTIONS
Quilting pencil or chalk
Stitch marker (optional)
Tapestry needle
1 1" (3cm) button

GAUGE
20 sts and 30 rows = 4" (10cm) in St st

KNITTING SKILLS
k2tog [knit 2 together]: Dec by knitting 2 sts
tog as 1 st (see page 22)
yo [yarn over]: Wrap the yarn once around the
right-hand needle and cont knitting; on the
subsequent row, treat the wrap as a st, creating an eyelet hole in the knitted fabric

EMBELLISHMENT SKILLS
Outline stitch (see page 32)

KNIT
CO 80 (88, 96) sts. Join for working in the rnd, being careful not to twist
sts. Place marker for beg of round, if desired.

Purl 1 rnd.

EYELET PATTERN

RND 1: Knit.

RND 2: *K6, yo, k2tog; rep from * to end.

RND 3: Knit.

RND 4: Knit.

RND 5: *K2, yo, k2tog, k4; rep from * to end.

RND 6: Knit.

Rep Rnds 1-6 once more, then Rnds 1-4 once.

Purl 1 rnd.

BO. Weave in ends.

EMBELLISH
Transfer the embellishment pattern below to the knitted fabric with a
quilting pencil or chalk. Using wool yarn and a tapestry needle, stitch
the embroidery pattern using outline stitch. Sew on a button where
indicated. Attach several strands of yarn to the headband behind
the button.

Pattern | *Template shown
at actual size*

- - - - - - - - edge of
knitted fabric

———— outline stitch

◯ eyelet

⊞ button

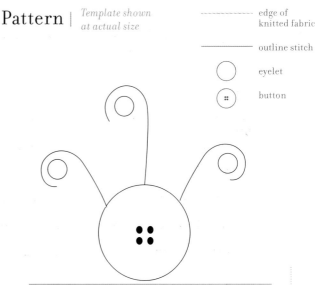

Fruit Punch Headband

I love this headband pattern. It is fast and simple, and it can be made with any yarn and any size needle—the larger the better. What I most enjoy, however, is combining different wools and seeing how they knit up together. I leave long tails at both ends of a headband so the wearer can trim them to whatever length she'd like. On my own headbands, I keep the tails long because they show off the yarn beautifully.

SIZES
Child M L/Adult S (Adult M-L)

FINISHED MEASUREMENTS
Length (not including ties): 14 (17)" 36 (43)cm
Width (at widest point): 4 (5½)" 10 (14)cm

YARN
Approximately 50 (70) yards 46 (64)m bulky
weight 100% wool yarn (A)
Approximately 50 (70) yards 46 (64)m
worsted weight 100% wool yarn (B)
*Shown: 2-ply thick-and-thin handspun
yarn, thrifted oddments*

NEEDLES
US 17 (12.75mm) straight needles
*If necessary, change needle size to obtain
correct gauge.*

NOTIONS
2 ⅝" (16mm) buttons

GAUGE
10 sts and 14 rows = 4" (10cm) in garter st with
yarn A and yarn B held together

KNITTING SKILLS
k2tog [knit 2 together]: Dec by knitting 2 sts
tog as 1 st (see page 22)
kfb [knit one front and back]: Inc by
knitting into front and back of next st
(see page 23)

KNIT
With yarn A and yarn B held together, CO 2 (2) sts, leaving a very
long tail (at least 30" [76cm]).

ROW 1: K1, kfb—3 sts.

ROW 2: K1, kfb, k1—4 sts.

ROW 3: Knit to last 2 sts, kfb, k1—5 sts.

Rep Row 3 5 (9) times more—10 (14) sts.

Work even in garter st until piece measures 11½ (13½)" 29 (34)cm.

NEXT ROW: Knit to last 3 sts, k2tog, k1—9 (13) sts.

Rep last row 7 (11) times more—2 sts.

Next row: K2tog.

Fasten off last st, leaving another very long tail.

EMBELLISH
Sew 2 ⅝" (16mm) buttons onto the edge of the headband.

Mittens

There are many ways to keep your hands warm, and I have included a few of those options in this chapter: mittens, wristers and fingerless mitts. And just as there are many ways to keep your hands warm, there are many ways to make the things that keep your hands warm. Accessories for the hands have some or all of the following elements: a cuff, a gusset and thumb, a palm and a decrease section. There are several options for each of these elements. The patterns that follow are but a smattering of different options.

For example, the cuff of a mitt or mitten can be snug or straight. A snug cuff, such as the one on the *Snow Day Mittens* on page 102, helps keep snow out of the mittens. A straight cuff, like the one on the *Tree Bud Mitts* on page 106, can be more comfortable to wear.

Gussets are one way of adding stitches to your knitting in order to create a thumb. You can also choose not to add a thumb to your piece, like I did with the *Night Sky Wristers* on page 104, or you could choose an afterthought thumb, like the one in the *Popsicle Mittens* on page 100. The most important thing to take into account when you make choices about how to begin a thumb is that you end up with a number of stitches that will fit around the thumb of the future wearer.

After the gusset, the palm section awaits. For wristers and mitts, this is the end of the line. The only decision left is how long to make the palm on your mitts. A long palm section, like the one I used on the *Communion Mitts* on page 108, can add extra warmth, but a short palm leaves your fingers free for extra dexterity. In mittens, the rule of thumb is to work the palm section until it reaches the tip of the pinky finger. After that, the decrease section of the mitten begins. These patterns show only one option for decreases: the three-part spiral decrease. There are many other choices, so check out my suggested reading if you'd like other options (see *Resources*, page 122).

Popsicle Mittens

These mittens, made from soft handspun merino, feel so good on the hands. The skeins of yarn I used for this project were dyed and spun so that they would be self-striping without color repeats. To mix things up a bit, I knit each mitten from a different end of the skein, resulting in reversed striping patterns on each mitten. I chose an afterthought thumb for these mittens because I love the way it fits my hand, and it also adds a bit of a traditional look and style to the mittens. I wanted the fabulous yarn I used to be the star of these mittens, so I chose simple, understated embellishments that match the sweet nature of this yarn.

SIZES

Adult S (M, L)

FINISHED MEASUREMENTS

Circumference: 7 (7½, 8¼)" 18 (19, 21)cm
Length: 9½ (9½, 10¼)" 24 (24, 26)cm

YARN

Approximately 120 (130, 145) yards 110 (119, 133)m heavy worsted or Aran weight 100% wool yarn
Small amount of 100% wool yarn for embellishment
Shown: handspun yarn by Feral Feminine, thrifted oddments

NEEDLES

Set of US 9 (5.5mm) dpns
If necessary, change needle size to obtain correct gauge.

NOTIONS

Quilting pencil or chalk
Scrap yarn
Tapestry needle
1 ¾" (2cm) button

GAUGE

19 sts and 30 rows = 4" (10cm) in St st

KNITTING SKILLS

k2tog [knit 2 together]: Dec by knitting 2 sts tog as 1 st (see page 22)

EMBELLISHMENT SKILLS

Outline stitch (see page 32)

Pattern | *Template shown at actual size*

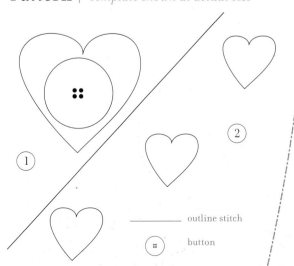

———— outline stitch

button

KNIT

CO 34 (36, 40) sts. Divide as evenly as possible over 3 dpns and join for working in the rnd, being careful not to twist sts.

Purl 1 rnd.

Change to St st and work even until piece measures 5 (5, 5)" 13 (13, 13)cm.

NEXT RND: Knit 2 sts. Drop main yarn and knit next 5 (6, 6) sts with scrap yarn. Slip these 5 (6, 6) sts back to the left-hand needle and knit them again with main yarn. Knit to end of round. (These sts will be used to make the thumb later, but for now, knit them like all the other sts.)

Continue in St st for a further 3½ (3½, 4)" 9 (9, 10)cm, or until mitten reaches tip of pinky finger. Dec 1 (0, 1) st at end of last rnd—33 (36, 39) sts.

TOP DECREASES

Distribute sts evenly over 3 dpns—11 (12, 13) sts per needle.

NEXT RND: *Knit to last 2 sts on needle, k2tog; rep from * to end—30 (33, 36) sts.

Knit 1 rnd.

Rep last 2 rnds once more—27 (30, 33) sts.

NEXT RND: *Knit to last 2 sts on needle, k2tog; rep from * to end—24 (27, 30) sts.

Rep last rnd 6 (7, 8) times more—6 (6, 6) sts.

Cut yarn, leaving a 6" (15cm) tail. Use tapestry needle to thread tail through rem sts, pull tight and fasten off. Weave in ends.

THUMB

Carefully remove scrap yarn. Place the 5 (6, 6) sts on top of the resulting hole on one dpn, and bottom 5 (6, 6) sts on another dpn. Join yarn and knit 1 rnd, picking up and knitting 1 st at each corner of the hole—12 (14, 14) sts. (See page 30 for instructions on picking up sts.)

Divide these sts as evenly as possible over 3 needles. Work even in St st for 2 (2, 2¼)" 5 (5, 6)cm.

NEXT RND: *K2 (1, 1), k2tog; rep from * 3 (4, 4) times, knit to end—9 (10, 10) sts.

Knit 1 rnd.

NEXT RND: *K1 (0, 0), k2tog; rep from * to end—6 (5, 5) sts.

Cut yarn, leaving a 6" (15cm) tail. Use tapestry needle to thread tail through rem sts, pull tight and fasten off. Weave in ends.

EMBELLISH

Transfer the embellishment patterns shown at left to the knitted fabric with a quilting pencil or chalk. Using wool yarn and a tapestry needle, stitch the embroidery pattern using outline stitch. Sew on a button where indicated.

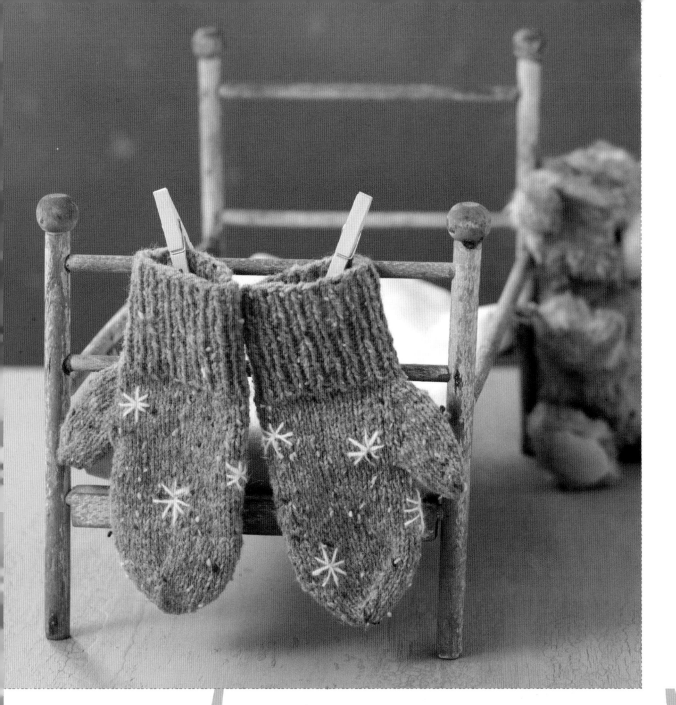

Snow Day Mittens

I wanted these mittens to be able to hold up against a day out playing in the snow. In order to make them warmer and more water resistant, I worked the worsted weight yarn on needles that were smaller than those usually recommended for the yarn weight. This created a thicker, firmer fabric than the recommended needle size would. Embroidering on these little mitts was a challenge because it was difficult to get my hands inside of them to work. If you have difficulty working on small items such as these, after making the first stitch from the inside of the item to the outside, work the rest of the stitches from the outside.

SIZES

Child M (L, XL)

6-18 mos. (4-6 years, 6-8 years)

FINISHED MEASUREMENTS

Palm circumference: 5½ (6, 6½)" 14 (15, 17)cm

Length: 6¼ (6¾, 7¼)" 16 (17, 18)cm

YARN

Approximately 80 (90, 100) yards 73 (82, 91)m worsted weight 100% wool yarn

Small amount of 100% wool yarn for embellishment

Shown: recycled sweater yarn, thrifted oddments

NEEDLES

Set of US 4 (3.5mm) dpns

If necessary, change needle size to obtain correct gauge.

NOTIONS

Scrap yarn

Stitch markers

Tapestry needle

GAUGE

24 sts and 36 rows = 4" (10cm) in St st

KNITTING SKILLS

M1L [make 1 left]: Inc by knitting into the bar between sts to create a new st that leans to the left (see page 24)

M1R [make 1 right]: Inc by knitting into the bar between sts to create a new st that leans to the right (see page 25)

k2tog [knit 2 together]: Dec by knitting 2 sts tog as 1 st (see page 22)

EMBELLISHMENT SKILLS

Single satin stitch (see page 32)

KNIT

CO 32 (36, 40) sts. Divide as evenly as possible over 3 dpns and join for working in the rnd, being careful not to twist sts.

RND 1: *K1, p1; rep from * to end.

Rep Rnd 1 until piece measures 2 (2¼, 2¼)" 5 (6, 6)cm from cast-on edge. Change to St st and knit 2 rnds.

THUMB GUSSET

NEXT RND: K15 (17, 19), pm, M1L, K1, M1R, pm, knit to end—34 (38, 42) sts; 3 sts between markers.

Knit 1 rnd.

NEXT RND: Knit to marker, sm, M1L, knit to marker, M1R, sm, knit to end—36 (40, 44) sts; 5 sts between markers.

Rep last 2 rnds 3 (4, 5) times—42 (48, 54) sts; 11 (13, 15) sts between markers.

Knit 1 rnd.

NEXT RND: Knit to marker, remove marker, slip next 11 (13, 15) sts onto scrap yarn. Remove second marker, CO 1 st over gap. (See page 19 for instructions on casting on backward-loop style.) Knit rem sts—32 (36, 40) sts.

Work even until piece measures 3¼ (3½, 4)" 8 (9, 10)cm from top of cuff, or until mitten reaches to tip of pinky finger.

TOP DECREASES

Redistribute sts over needles—11 (12, 13) sts on first needle, 11 (12, 13) sts on second needle, 10 (12, 14) sts on third needle.

DEC RND: *Knit to last 2 sts on needle, k2tog; rep from * to end—29 (33, 37) sts.

Knit 1 rnd.

Rep last 2 rnds twice more—23 (27, 31) sts.

Rep Dec Rnd only 6 (7, 8) times more—5 (6, 7) sts.

Cut yarn, leaving a 6" (15cm) tail. Use tapestry needle to thread tail through rem sts, pull tight and fasten off.

THUMB

Place 11 (13, 15) sts from scrap yarn onto dpns. Knit 1 rnd, picking up and knitting 1 st over gap—12 (14, 16) sts. (See page 30 for instructions on picking up sts.) Work even in St st for ¾ (1, 1¼)" 2 (3, 3)cm.

NEXT RND: *K2, k2tog; rep from * to end, end with k2tog for size M—9 (10, 12) sts.

Knit 1 rnd.

NEXT RND: K1 (0, 0), *k2tog; rep from * to end—5 (5, 6) sts.

Cut yarn, leaving a 6" (15cm) tail. Use tapestry needle to thread tail through rem sts, pull tight and fasten off. Weave in ends. If there are any holes where the thumb meets the hand, use your yarn tail to close them.

EMBELLISH

Randomly embroider eight-pointed stars over the mittens using single satin stitch.

Night Sky Wristers

This pattern was inspired by a Red Cross knitting pattern from World War I. I could never understand why wristers were so popular in modern times, but finding this vintage pattern got me thinking that there really must be a point to them. After knitting and wearing a pair, I'm a convert. Wristers really do make you warmer—probably because they cover more body with warm fiber, and they prevent drafts from going up your coat sleeves. Warmth aside, these lovelies are gloriously funky and would be beautiful sticking out underneath your favorite sweater any time of the year. I recommend choosing yarns that have a high amount of contrast in texture and shape for a fun look like these have.

sizes

Adult S (M, L)

finished measurements

Circumference: 6 (7, 8)" 15 (18, 20)cm
Length: 9 (9, 9)" 23 (23, 23)cm

yarn

Approximately 50 (60, 65) yards 46 (55, 59)m
chunky weight wool blend yarn (A)
Approximately 50 (60, 75) yards 46 (55, 59)m
worsted weight 100% wool yarn (B)
Small amount of 100% wool yarn for
embellishment

*Shown: handspun yarn by Rachel-Marie,
thrifted oddments*

needles

US 10½ (6.5mm) straight needles
*If necessary, change needle size to obtain
correct gauge.*

notions

Tapestry needle
US G (4.5mm) or H (5mm) crochet hook

gauge

16 sts and 21 rows = 4" (10cm) in Stripe Patt

embellishment skills

Crochet chain edging (see page 34)

KNIT

STRIPE PATTERN

Switch between yarn A and yarn B at random intervals.

Do not cut color not in use, but carry it up the side of the work.

CUFF

CO 26 (30, 34) sts.

Randomly changing between rows of knit stitches and rows of purl stitches, work until piece measures 9 (9, 9)" 23 (23, 23)cm from cast-on edge.

BO.

Weave in ends.

Fold knitted fabric in half lengthwise. Whipstitch seam closed to approx 3 (3, 3)" 8 (8, 8)cm from top edge. Leave a gap of approx 1½-2" (4-5 cm) open for the thumbhole, then seam the top 1-1½" (3-4cm) closed.

Weave in ends.

EMBELLISH

Using wool yarn, work a crochet chain edging around the thumbhole of each wrister. Work lines of crochet chain stitches on the backs of the wristers as desired.

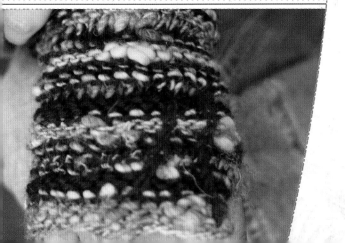

Tree Bud Mitts

Although he's not so fond of full mittens, my husband can always use another pair of these mitts. He uses them when he goes out to smoke his pipe, when he plays the organ in drafty churches and for biking around the city. I wear my own pair daily during the colder seasons, pulling my hands up inside of them when my fingers get cold. With mittens, and especially with fingerless mitts, I find that I'm not as picky about size. There's something about big warm mittens that make me very happy, and for that reason, I would easily wear a large pair of these mitts on my women's-size-medium hands.

SIZES

Adult S (M, L)

FINISHED MEASUREMENTS

Circumference: 6 (7¼, 8¼)" 15 (18, 21)cm
Length: 8 (8, 8)" 20 (20, 20)cm

YARN

Approximately 55 (65, 75) yards 51 (59, 69)m
worsted weight wool/mohair blend yarn (A)
Approximately 55 (65, 75) yards 51 (59, 69)m
worsted weight 100% wool yarn (B)
Small amounts of 100% wool yarn in 2 colors
for embellishment
*Shown: recycled sweater yarn, Brown Sheep
Lamb's Pride Worsted, thrifted oddments*

NEEDLES

Set of US 7 (4.5mm) dpns
*If necessary, change needle size to obtain
correct gauge.*

NOTIONS

Quilting pencil or chalk
Scrap yarn
Stitch markers
Tapestry needle

GAUGE

21 sts and 32 rows = 4" (10cm) in St st

KNITTING SKILLS

M1L [make 1 left]: Inc by knitting into the
bar between sts to create a new st that leans to
the left (see page 24)
M1R [make 1 right]: Inc by knitting into the
bar between sts to create a new st that leans to
the right (see page 25)

EMBELLISHMENT SKILLS

Outline stitch (see page 32)
Single satin stitch (see page 32)

KNIT

STRIPE PATTERN

4 rnds yarn A

4 rnds yarn B

Do not cut color not in use, but carry it up the inside of the work.

CUFF

With yarn A, CO 32 (38, 44) sts. Divide as evenly as possible over 3 dpns and join for working in the rnd, being careful not to twist sts.

*Purl 1 rnd. Knit 1 rnd. Rep from * once more.

Change to St st and Stripe Patt and work even until piece measures 3 (3, 3)" 8 (8, 8)cm from cast-on edge.

THUMB GUSSET

NEXT RND: K15 (18, 21), pm, M1L, k1, M1R, pm, knit to end—34 (40, 46) sts; 3 sts between markers.

Knit 1 rnd.

INC RND: *Knit to marker, sm, M1L, knit to marker, M1R, sm, knit to end—36 (42, 48) sts; 5 sts between markers.

Rep Inc Rnd on every 4th rnd 4 (3, 3) times—44 (48, 54)sts; 13 (11, 11) sts between markers.

Rep Inc Rnd on every 3rd rnd 1 (3, 3) time—46 (54, 60)sts; 15 (17, 17) sts between markers.

NEXT RND: Knit to marker, remove marker, slip next 15 (17, 17) sts onto scrap yarn. Remove second marker, CO 1 st over gap. (See page 19 for instructions on casting on backward-loop style.) Knit rem sts—32 (38, 44) sts.

Work even until piece measures approx. 7½ (7½, 7½)" 19 (19, 19)cm ending with a stripe in yarn B complete. Change to yarn A.

*Knit 1 rnd. Purl 1 rnd. Rep from * once more.

BO.

THUMB

Place 15 (17, 17) sts from scrap yarn on dpns. Join appropriate color yarn and knit 1 rnd, picking up and knitting 1 st over the gap—16 (18, 18) sts. (See page 30 for instructions on picking up sts.)

Work even in St st for about ½ (½, ½)" 1 (1, 1)cm, or until the current stripe is complete. Change colors, if desired.

*Knit 1 rnd. Purl 1 rnd. Rep from * once more.

BO.

Weave in ends. If there are any holes where the thumb meets the hand, use your yarn tail to close them.

EMBELLISH

Transfer the embellishment pattern on page 124 to the knitted fabric with a quilting pencil or chalk. Using wool yarn and a tapestry needle, stitch the embroidery pattern using outline stitch and single satin stitch.

Pattern | *see page 124*

Communion Mitts

There is something very classy, fun and dressed-up about long fingerless mitts that makes me want to wear them all of the time. And for warmth, you can't beat this pair that goes far up your arm and down over your fingers. Also, the flexible ribbing on this pair can be folded back to give you more maneuverability with your hands, or left down to give you more warmth. If you'd like a more secure ribbing, try using a k2, p2 ribbing at the cuff and fingers instead of k3, p1 ribbing. This will provide a tighter ribbing that will hold everything in place.

SIZES

Adult S (M, L)

FINISHED MEASUREMENTS

Palm circumference: 6½ (7¼, 8)" 17 (18, 20)cm
Length: 14 (15, 15)" 36 (38, 38)cm

YARN

Approximately 180 (220, 240) yards 165 (201, 219)m worsted weight wool blend yarn
Small amount of 100% wool yarn for embellishment

Shown: wool/nylon blend recycled sweater yarn

NEEDLES

Set of US 8 (5mm) dpns

If necessary, change needle size to obtain correct gauge.

NOTIONS

Quilting pencil or chalk
Scrap yarn
Stitch markers
Tapestry needle
4 ½" (13mm) buttons

GAUGE

20 sts and 30 rows = 4" (10cm) in St st

KNITTING SKILLS

M1L [make 1 left]: Inc by knitting into the bar between sts to create a new st that leans to the left (see page 24)

M1R [make 1 right]: Inc by knitting into the bar between sts to create a new st that leans to the right (see page 25)

k2tog [knit 2 together]: Dec by knitting 2 sts tog as 1 st (see page 22)

EMBELLISHMENT SKILLS

Outline stitch (see page 32)

KNIT

CO 40 (44, 48) sts. Divide sts as evenly as possible over 3 dpns and join for working in the rnd, being careful not to twist sts.

RND 1: *K3, p1; rep from * to end.

Rep Rnd 1 until piece measures 2½ (2½, 2½)" 6 (6, 6)cm.

Change to St st and work even until piece measures 4½ (5, 5)" 11 (13, 13)cm from cast-on edge.

NEXT RND: *K8 (9, 10), k2tog; rep from * to end—36 (40, 44) sts.

Work even until piece measures 7 (8, 8)" 18 (20, 20)cm from cast-on edge.

NEXT RND: *K7 (8, 9), k2tog; rep from * to end—32 (36, 40) sts.

Work even until piece measures 9 (10, 10)" 23 (25, 25)cm from cast-on edge.

THUMB GUSSET

NEXT RND: K15 (17, 19), pm, M1L, k1, M1R, pm, knit to end—34 (38, 42) sts; 3 sts between markers.

Knit 2 rnds.

INC RND: Knit to marker, sm, M1L, knit to marker, M1R, sm, knit to end—36 (40, 44) sts; 5 sts between markers.

Rep Inc Rnd on every 3rd rnd once more, then on every 4th rnd twice more—42 (46, 50)sts; 11 sts between markers.

Knit 1 rnd.

NEXT RND: Knit to marker, remove marker, slip next 11 sts onto scrap yarn. Remove second marker, CO 1 st over gap. (See page 19 for instructions on casting on backward-loop style.) Knit rem sts—32 (36, 40) sts.

Work even in St st until piece measures 12 (13, 13)" 30 (33, 33)cm from cast-on edge.

NEXT RND: *K3, p1; rep from * to end.

Rep last rnd until piece measures 14 (15, 15)" 36 (38, 38)cm from cast-on edge.

BO in patt.

THUMB

Place 11 sts from scrap yarn on dpns. Knit 1 rnd, picking up and knitting 1 st over gap—12 sts.

NEXT RND: *K3, p1; rep from * to end.

Rep last rnd until ribbing measures 1 (1, 1)" 3 (3, 3)cm.

BO in patt.

Weave in ends. If there are any holes where the thumb meets the hand, use your yarn tail to close them.

EMBELLISH

Transfer the embellishment pattern on page 126 to the knitted fabric with a quilting pencil or chalk. Using wool yarn and a tapestry needle, stitch the embroidery pattern using outline stitch. Sew on buttons where indicated.

Pattern | *see page 126*

Scarves

There are so many options available when designing scarves; these popular accessories are endlessly customizable. You can create different lengths, widths and even shapes to suit every taste and style. From the traditional wrap-around-and-around *All-Star Scarf* on page 120 to the fun and funky asymmetrical *Flutter Neck Scarf* on page 118, the patterns in this chapter will keep your neck warm and toasty. Plus, scarves are a great canvas for special embellishments. Fringe is a wonderful way to highlight special yarns. And because fit is not as much of an issue with scarves as it is with hats or mittens, you can experiment with new embellishment techniques, such as appliqué, like I did on the *All-Star Scarf* on page 120.

The most important choice you'll make when designing your own scarves is the fiber you select. Yarns that I don't find the least bit itchy become itchy when I put them flush to my neck and leave them there. Make sure to use only your softest yarns for these patterns; you'll be much happier with your results.

Moon over Waves Scarf

I reserve this scarf pattern for the softest recycled sweater yarns that would feel coziest wrapped around the neck. I also often use small balls of unique yarn left over from other projects for the embroidery and fringe. The fringe on this scarf is an especially good way to show off a wonderful yarn. When embroidering on this scarf, consider an allover pattern that covers much of the width, rather than something more central. A wide embroidery pattern can help stop the curliness of the edges.

SIZES
One size

FINISHED MEASUREMENTS
Length (not including fringe): 40" (1m)
Width (unrolled): 5" (13cm)

YARN
Approximately 110 yards (101m) worsted
weight mohair/nylon/wool blend yarn
Small amount of 100% wool yarn for
embellishment
Shown: recycled sweater yarn,
thrifted oddments

NEEDLES
US 10½ (6.5mm) straight needles
If necessary, change needle size to obtain
correct gauge.

NOTIONS
Quilting pencil or chalk
Tapestry needle
US G (4.5mm) or H (5mm) crochet hook

GAUGE
16 sts and 21 rows = 4" (10cm) in St st with
yarn doubled

EMBELLISHMENT SKILLS
Outline stitch (see page 32)
Creating decorative fringe (see page 35)

KNIT
With yarn doubled, CO 20 sts.

Beginning with a purl row, work even in St st until piece measures
40" (1m) or desired length.

BO.

Weave in ends.

EMBELLISH
Transfer the embellishment pattern below to the knitted fabric with a
quilting pencil or chalk. Using wool yarn and a tapestry needle, stitch the
embroidery pattern using outline stitch. Attach a fringe of wool yarn to
the other end of the scarf.

Pattern | *Template shown*
at actual size

end of scarf

outline stitch

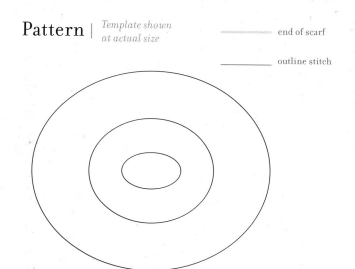

Snuggly Neck Scarf

This project started with a ball of soft, squishy thick-and-thin handspun merino wool. My goal was to make a little scarf that felt like a big scarf, but without the heaviness. I also wanted to show off the yarn and be able to fit fairly large buttons through the knitting so that the scarf would be adjustable. If you have buttons in mind for this project, make sure you knit at a gauge that will allow your buttons to fit through the knitted fabric. Otherwise, I recommend doing the knitting first, then getting out the button stash and finding the right button for the fabric. This scarf is so easy to make, but also so satisfying to wear. And, if you ever decide to try your hand at spinning, this is a great project for the first yarn you create on your drop spindle!

SIZES
One size

FINISHED MEASUREMENTS
Length (unbuttoned): 15" (38cm)
Width: 7" (18cm)

YARN
Approximately 50 yards (46m) bulky weight
100% wool yarn
Shown: thick-and-thin handspun yarn

NEEDLES
US 17 (12.75mm) straight needles
If necessary, change needle size to obtain correct gauge.

NOTIONS
Tapestry needle
2 1" (3cm) buttons

GAUGE
10 sts and 18 rows = 4" (10cm) in garter st

KNIT
CO 18 sts.

Work in garter st until piece measures 15" (38cm), or desired length.

BO all sts.

Weave in ends.

EMBELLISH
Sew 2 1" (3cm) buttons onto a short edge of the neck scarf.

Silky Smoke Ring

I learned about smoke rings from my mother-in-law. She loves this type of scarf because it is so versatile, doesn't flatten her hair and keeps her warm during the long Alaskan winters. A smoke ring can be worn around the neck as a scarf, or over the head as a hood. Although smoke rings are often lacy, I chose to make this one out of a solid fabric for extra warmth. For comfort, I also chose a yarn that drapes well and knit it loosely on larger needles. The loose gauge allows the clip-on earring to slide through the fabric easily so that the smoke ring can be adjusted to fit snuggly.

sizes

One size

FINISHED Measurements

Circumference: 22" (56cm)

Height: 13½" (34cm)

yarn

Approximately 210 yards (192m) worsted weight alpaca/silk blend yarn

Shown: Cascade Success

Needles

16" (40cm) US 9 (5.5mm) circular needle

If necessary, change needle size to obtain correct gauge.

NOTIONS

Stitch marker

Tapestry needle

Clip-on earring or brooch

Gauge

18 sts and 24 rows = 4" (10cm) in St st

KNIT

CO 100 sts. Join for working in the rnd, being careful not to twist sts. Place marker for beg of rnd, if desired.

BORDER

*Purl 1 rnd. Knit 1 rnd. Rep from * once more.

Knit 2 rnds.

NEXT RND: *K1, p1; rep from * to end.

PATTERN

RNDS 1–3: Knit.

RND 4: *K3, p1; rep from * to end.

RNDS 5–7: Knit.

RND 8: K1, *p1, k3; rep from * to last 3 sts, p1, k2.

Rep Rnds 1–8 7 times more, then Rnds 1–7 once more.

BORDER

Purl 1 rnd. Knit 1 rnd. Purl 1 rnd.

BO.

Weave in ends.

EMBELLISH

Attach a clip-on earring or brooch to the knitted fabric.

Flutter Neck Scarf

This neck scarf went through several shaping incarnations before I found one that I liked. It starts as a straight strip that goes around the neck, and then one side flares out. The unusual shaping of this scarf gives it a unique look. For embellishing, I focused on using buttons as both decorations and as a fastener. Have fun finding just the right buttons; try all sorts of different colors, sizes and shapes. If you are in search of great buttons, check your local thrift stores. If you live in a city, you may also have an amazing button shop close by.

SIZES
One size

FINISHED MEASUREMENTS
Length: 18½" (47cm)
Width (at widest point): 7¾" (20cm)

YARN
Approximately 55 yards (50m) worsted weight
100% wool yarn
Shown: recycled sweater yarn

NEEDLES
US 10½ (6.5mm) straight needles
*If necessary, change needle size to obtain
correct gauge.*

NOTIONS
Tapestry needle
1 1¼" (3cm) button
4 ½" (13mm) buttons

GAUGE
16 sts and 21 rows = 4" (10cm) in St st
with yarn doubled

KNITTING SKILLS
kfb [knit one front and back]: Inc by
knitting into front and back of next st
(see page 23)

KNIT
With yarn doubled, CO 16 sts.

ROW 1 (WS): K2, p12, k2.

ROW 2 (RS): Knit.

Rep Rows 1–2 until piece measures 12½" (32cm) from cast-on edge,
ending with Row 1.

NEXT ROW (RS): K2, kfb, knit to end—17 sts.

NEXT ROW (WS): K2, purl to last 2 sts, k2.

Rep last 2 rows 11 times more, ending with WS row—28 sts.

NEXT ROW (RS): Knit.

NEXT ROW (WS): K2, purl to last 2 sts, k2.

NEXT ROW (RS): K2, kfb, knit to end—29 sts.

NEXT ROW (WS): K2, purl to last 2 sts, k2.

Rep last 4 rows twice more—31 sts.

NEXT ROW (RS): Knit.

NEXT ROW (WS): K2, purl to last 2 sts, k2.

BO.

Weave in ends. Block lightly.

EMBELLISH
Sew 4 ½" (13cm) buttons along the increasing edge of the wide
end of the neck scarf. Sew the 1¼" (3cm) button in the middle
of the wide end of the neck scarf. Braid three strands of yarn
together to form a 6" (15cm) cord. Attach the braided cord to the
narrow end of the neck scarf, forming a button loop.

All-Star Scarf

I am not yet brave enough with my limited knowledge of fabric to appliqué onto a knit fabric that needs to stretch (like my hats), so scarves are a great place to start. For this appliqué, I found a vintage napkin at the thrift store, cut it to a size that complemented the scarf's width, hemmed it and attached it to the scarf with blanket stitch. In essence, without the fancy edge stitch, I did the exact same thing that I did throughout high school to patch my jeans. I found out while working on this scarf that it is much easier to embroider precise forms, like stars, onto woven fabric than knitted fabric. I'd been trying to embroider stars on my knitting for a long time—and finally succeeded via this route. Consider using an appliqué base for your embroidery if you want to embellish your knits with complex designs.

SIZES
One size

FINISHED MEASUREMENTS
Length: 56" (140cm)
Width: 4½" (11cm)

YARN
Approximately 260 yards (238m) worsted weight angora/wool blend yarn
Small amounts of 100% wool yarn in 2 colors for embellishment
Shown: Berroco Pleasure, thrifted oddments

NEEDLES
US 10½ (6.5mm) straight needles
If necessary, change needle size to obtain correct gauge.

NOTIONS
Quilting pencil or chalk
Sewing needle with a large eye
Thread to match fabric
3½" × 4" (9cm × 10cm) piece of fabric

GAUGE
18 sts and 26 rows = 4" (10cm) in garter st

EMBELLISHMENT SKILLS
Blanket stitch (see page 32)
Running stitch (see page 32)

KNIT
CO 20 sts.

Work in garter st for 56" (1.4m), or to desired length.

BO.

Weave in ends.

EMBELLISH
Hem the piece of fabric and attach it to one end of the scarf with blanket stitch. Transfer the embellishment pattern below to the fabric patch with a quilting pencil or chalk. Using thin wool yarn and a sewing needle with a large eye, stitch the embroidery pattern using running stitch.

Pattern | *Template shown at actual size*   — — — running stitch

Resources

I highly recommend looking for yarn at craft shows, farmer's markets and other local events. Buying locally contributes to your local economy and also gives your knitting an interesting flair. All of the lovely people whose goods I have used in this book have shops online at www.etsy.com, as do I. If you can't find much locally, or even if you can and want to diversify like I do, there are many many amazing crafters selling their wares on the Internet. Look on Etsy or run an Internet search for handspun or hand-dyed yarn. You are sure to find pages and pages of inspiration and temptation.

YARN

Daniela Kloppman FeltStudio
www.feltstudio.co.uk
All Things Grow Hat (see page 76), 1970s Ski Sweater Hat (see page 80) and Yellow Bells Jester Hat (see page 86)

Feral Feminine
www.feralfeminine.etsy.com
Twirly Girl Bonnet (see page 88) and Popsicle Mittens (see page 100)

Rachel-Marie
www.knittydirtygirl.com
Night Sky Wristers (see page 104)

EMBELLISHMENTS

Mwah! Creations
www.mwahcreations.etsy.com
Daffodil Headband (see page 92)

Scatterbox Originals
www.scatterboxoriginals.etsy.com
Daffodil Headband (see page 92)

Vintage Necessities
www.vintagenecessities.etsy.com
Fruit Punch Headband (see page 96)

BOOKS

These are the books that I would wish upon any fiber artist. They're the kind of books that say, "Come on, design your own!" That said, I do not recommend working only from these. Try joining a knitting or fiber art guild near you. There is so much to learn—new ingenious techniques, old ingenious techniques—and I really believe that we all have something to share with one another. I recommend a good diet of both your own creative endeavors and those of others. Sharing new ideas and learning new techniques will not only help you join in the conversations in the larger community and expand your horizons, but will also help to give you the confidence to try creating your own new fresh and interesting designs.

The Knitter's Handy Book of Patterns: Basic Designs in Multiple Sizes & Gauges
Ann Budd, Interweave Press, August 2002

A Treasury of Knitting Patterns
Barbara G. Walker, Schoolhouse Press, May 1998

The Twisted Sisters Sock Workbook: Dyeing, Painting, Spinning, Designing, Knitting
Lynne Vogel, Interweave Press, October 2002

Spin It: Making Yarn from Scratch
Lee Raven and Traci Bunkers, Interweave Press, May 2003

The Dyer's Companion
Dagmar Klos, Interweave Press, April 2005

KNITTING NEEDLE CONVERSIONS

diameter (mm)	US size	suggested yarn weight
2	0	Lace Weight
2.25	1	Lace and Fingering Weight
2.75	2	Lace and Fingering Weight
3.25	3	Fingering and Sport Weight
3.5	4	Fingering and Sport Weight
3.75	5	DK and Sport Weight
4	6	DK, Sport and Aran/Worsted Weight
4.5	7	Aran/Worsted Weight
5	8	Aran/Worsted and Heavy Worsted Weight
5.5	9	Aran/Worsted, Heavy Worsted and Chunky/Bulky
6	10	Chunky/Bulky
6.5	10½	Chunky/Bulky and Super Bulky
8	11	Chunky/Bulky and Super Bulky
9	13	Super Bulky
10	15	Super Bulky
12.75	17	Super Bulky
15	19	Super Bulky
20	36	Super Bulky

KNITTING ABBREVIATIONS

approx	approximately
beg	begin(ning)
BO	bind off
CO	cast on
cont	continu(e)(ing)
dec	decreas(e)(ing)
dpn(s)	double-pointed needle(s)
foll	follow(s)(ing)
inc	increas(e)(ing)
k	knit
kfb	knit one front and back
k2tog	knit 2 together
M1L	make one left
M1R	make one right
p	purl
pm	place marker
p2tog	purl 2 together
psso	pass slipped stitch over
rem	remaining
RS	right side
rep	repeat
sl	slip
sm	slip marker
SSK	slip, slip, knit
st(s)	stitch(es)
St st	Stockinette stitch
work 2 tog	work 2 together
WS	wrong side
yo	yarn over

YARN WEIGHT GUIDELINES

Since the names given to different weights of yarn can vary widely depending on the country of origin or the yarn manufacturer's preference, The Craft Yarn Council of America has put together a standard yarn weight system to impose a bit of order on the sometimes unruly yarn labels. Look for a picture of a skein of yarn with a number 0–6 on most kinds of yarn to figure out its "official" weight. Gauge is given over 4" (10cm) of Stockinette stitch. The information in the chart below is taken from www.yarnstandards.com.

	SUPER BULKY (6)	BULKY (5)	MEDIUM (4)	LIGHT (3)	FINE (2)	SUPERFINE (1)	LACE (0)
Also Includes	bulky, roving	chunky, craft, rug	worsted, afghan, aran	dk, light, worsted	sport, baby	sock, fingering, baby	fingering, baby 10 count crochet thread
Gauge Over 4" (10cm)	6–11 sts	12–15 sts	16–20 sts	21–24 sts	23–26 sts	27–32 sts	33–40 sts
recommended needle size	11 and larger	9 to 11	7 to 9	5 to 7	3 to 5	1 to 3	000 to 1

SUBSTITUTING YARNS

If you substitute yarn, be sure to select a yarn of the same weight as the yarn recommended for the project. Even after checking that the recommended gauge on the yarn you plan to substitute is the same as for the yarn listed in the pattern, make sure to swatch and see. Use the chart above as a general guideline for selecting a yarn to substitute.

patterns

Berry Bramble Hat | page 56

- bottom of earflap
- outline stitch
- ∷ button

enlarge template by 200% to bring to full size

Back Alley Hat | page 70

- brim
- outline stitch

enlarge template by 167% to bring to full size

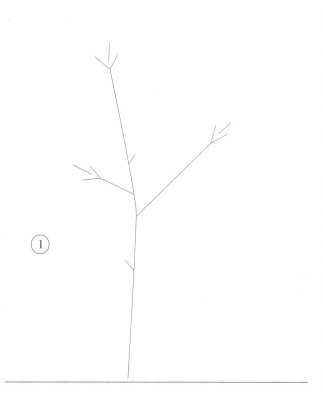

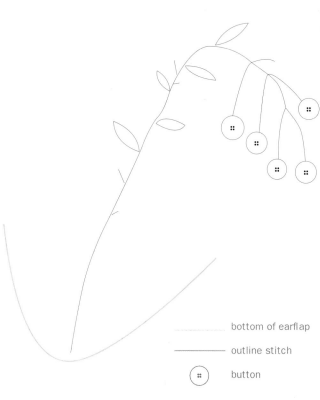

Tree Bud Mitts | page 106

- top of garter stitch
- outline stitch

enlarge template by 167% to bring to full size

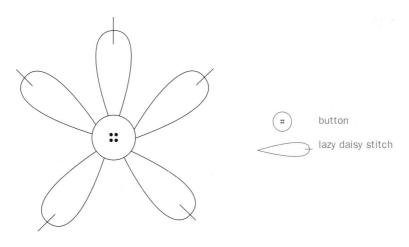

Daisy Helmet Hat | *Template shown at actual size*
page 84

button

lazy daisy stitch

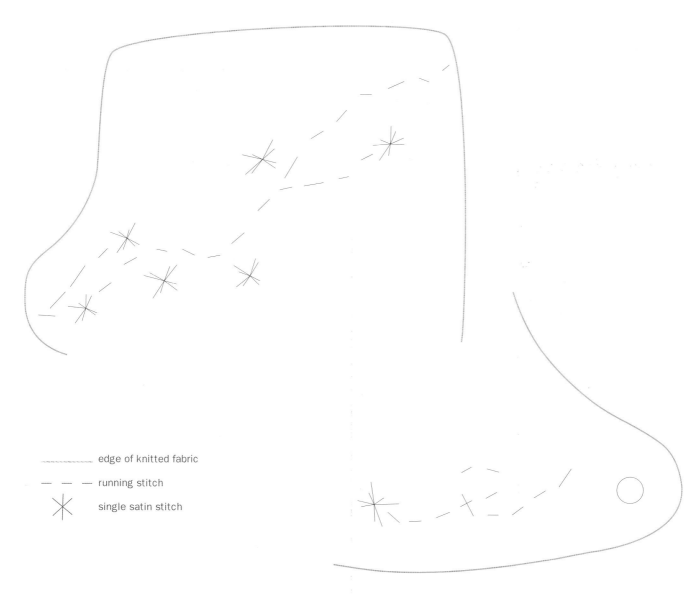

edge of knitted fabric

— — — running stitch

single satin stitch

Butterfly Pixie Bonnet | *enlarge template by 200% to bring to full size*
page 90

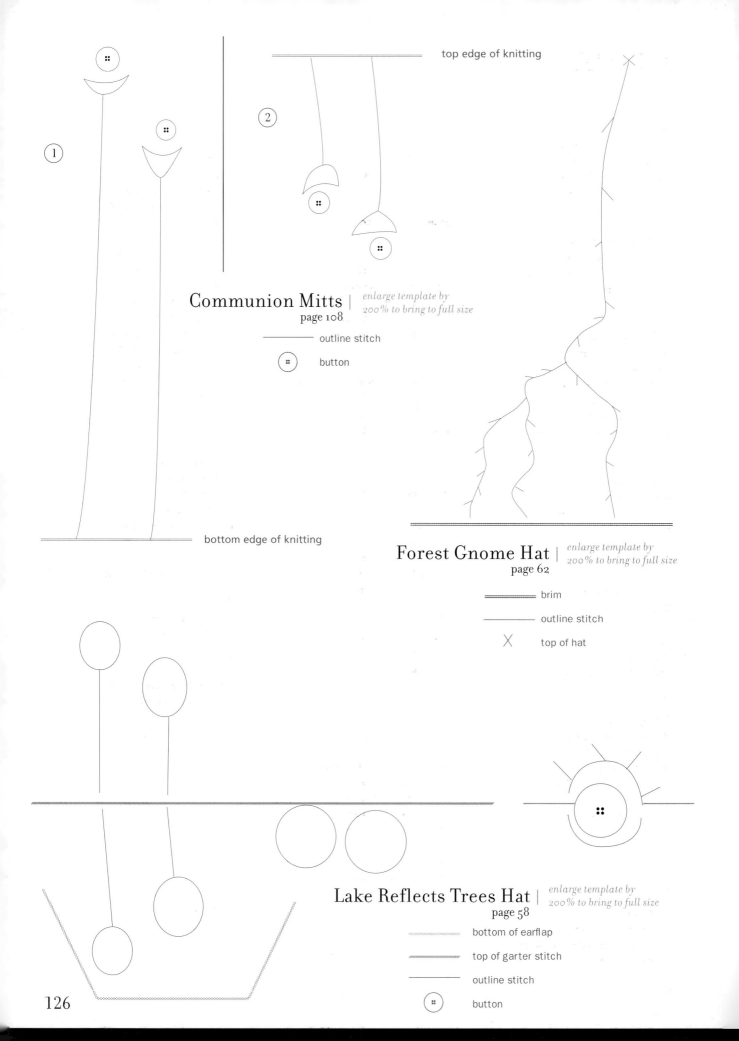

top edge of knitting

① ②

Communion Mitts | *enlarge template by 200% to bring to full size*
page 108

——— outline stitch

⊞ button

bottom edge of knitting

Forest Gnome Hat | *enlarge template by 200% to bring to full size*
page 62

══════ brim

——— outline stitch

✕ top of hat

Lake Reflects Trees Hat | *enlarge template by 200% to bring to full size*
page 58

∿∿∿∿∿ bottom of earflap

▨▨▨▨▨ top of garter stitch

——— outline stitch

⊞ button

index

A

abbreviations, list of, 123
All-Star Scarf, 120–121
All Things Grow Hat, 76-77
Apple on the Tree Hat, 64–65

B

Back Alley Hat, 70–71, 124
backward loop cast on, 19
Berry Bramble Hat, 56–57, 124
Biker Hat, 82–83
binding off, 26–27
blanket stitch, 32
blocking knits, 35
Blooming Tulips Hat, 50–51
bonnets,
    Butterfly Pixie Bonnet 90–91, 125
    Twirly Girl Bonnet 88–89
burn test for yarn, 11
Butterfly Pixie Bonnet, 90–91, 125

C

casting on, 18–19
color, 36–38
Communion Mitts, 108–109, 126
crochet edging, 34
Cupcake Hat, 46–47

D

Daffodil Headband, 92–93
Daisy Helmet Hat, 84–85, 125

E

embellishing, 39–40
embroidery on knitting, 39–40

F

fitting hats, 41
Flapper Eyelet Headband, 94–95
Flutter Neck Scarf, 118–119
Forest Gnome Hat, 62–63
Fresh Cut Grass Hat, 60–61
fringe, 35
Fruit Punch Headband, 96–97

G

gauge, 12

H

headbands
    Daffodil Headband, 92–93
    Flapper Eyelet Headband, 94–95
    Fruit Punch Headband, 96–97

I

I-cord, 31
increasing and decreasing, 22–25

J

joining stitches, 20–21

K

Kitchener stitch, 28–29
knit one front and back (kfb), 23
knitting abbreviations, 123
knitting continental, 19
knit two together (k2tog), 22

L

Lake Reflects Trees Hat, 56–57, 126
lazy daisy stitch, 33
Little Flower Top Hat, 44–45
Lollipop Hat, 52–53
long-tail cast on, 18

M

make one left (M1L), 24
make one right (M1R), 24
mittens
    Popsicle Mittens, 100–101
    Snow Day Mittens, 102–103
Moon Over Waves Scarf, 112–113
Mountain Sunset Inside Out Hat, 54–55

N

Nautical Nellie Hat, 78–79
Night Sky Wristers, 104–105
notions, 17

O

outline stitch, 32

P

pass slipped stitch over (psso), 22
picking up stitches, 30
planning a project, 36–41
Popsicle Mittens, 100–101
purling continental, 20

R

recycling sweaters, 10–15
Root Vegetable Hat, 68–69
running stitch, 32

S

scarves
    All-Star Scarf, 120–121
    Flutter Neck Scarf, 118–119
    Moon Over Waves Scarf, 112–113
    Silky Smoke Ring, 116–117
    Snuggly Neck Scarf, 114–115
Silky Smoke Ring, 116–117
single satin stitch, 32
sizing hats, 41
Ski Sweater Hat, 80–81
slip, slip, knit (SSK), 22
Snow Day Mittens, 102–103
Snow Princess Hat, 72–73
Snuggly Neck Scarf, 114
sweater recycling, 10-15
Sweet Pea Hat, 66–67

T

tassels, 35
techniques, 18–35
three-needle bind off, 27
tools, 16–17
Tree Bud Mitts, 106–107, 124
Twirly Girl Bonnet, 88–89

U

unraveling knitted fabric, 14

W

Wood and Water Hat, 48–49

Y

yarn substituting, 123
yarn weight guidelines, 123
Yellow Bells Jester Hat, 86–87

INDULGE YOUR CREATIVE SIDE
WITH THESE OTHER GREAT TITLES
FROM NORTH LIGHT BOOKS

SOFT AND SIMPLE KNITS FOR LITTLE ONES
Heidi Boyd

Learn to knit simple, adorable projects for the little ones in your life using the basic techniques taught in this book. *Soft and Simple Knits for Little Ones* includes patterns for clothing, accessories and toys that can be knit for last-minute gifts or for nearly instant gratification. Even if you've never picked up a set of knitting needles, author Heidi Boyd will teach you the skills needed to quickly and successfully complete each of the projects in this book without spending too much money or too much time.

ISBN-10: 1-58180-965-4
ISBN-13: 978-1-58180-965-7
paperback
160 pages
Z0696

YARNPLAY AT HOME
Lisa Shobhana Mason

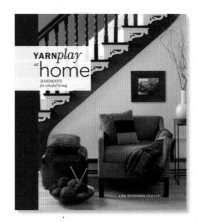

Lisa Shobhana Mason, author of *YarnPlay*, puts her colorful spin on handknits for the home in *YarnPlay at Home*. Filled with 25 stylish and simple projects for every room in the house, this book is perfect for knitters of all skill levels. Take a break from sweaters, hats and scarves and find unique pieces for every room in the house, and for every member of the family, including blankets, dishcloths and cozies. These colorful and cozy handknits make it easy to put your personal style stamp on your home.

ISBN-10: 1-60061-005-6
ISBN-13: 978-1-60061-005-9
paperback
128 pages
Z1001

CLOSELY KNIT
Hannah Fettig

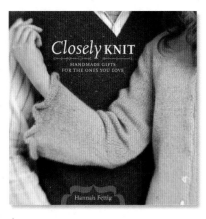

Closely Knit is filled with thoughtful knitted gifts to fit all the people you love: special handknits for mothers, daughters, sisters, the men in your life, precious wee ones and treasured friends. From luxurious scarves and wearable sweaters to cozy socks and even a quick-to-knit heart pin, there really is something for everyone on your list in this book. Projects range from quick and simple to true labors of love, and each is rated with a handy time guide so you can choose what to knit based on how much time you have. Bonus quick-fix options will save the day when you need to whip up a meaningful gift in a jiffy.

ISBN-10: 1-60061-018-8
ISBN-13: 978-1-60061-018-9
paperback
128 pages
Z1280

FITTED KNITS
Stephanie Japel

Fitted Knits features 25 projects to fit and flatter. You'll learn how to tailor t-shirts, sweaters, cardigans, coats and even a skirt and a dress to fit you perfectly. Take the guesswork out of knitting garments that fit. The book includes a detailed section that shows you how to know when and where increases and decreases should be placed to create the most attractive shaping.

ISBN-10: 1-58180-872-0
ISBN-13: 978-1-58180-872-8
paperback
144 pages
Z0574

These books and other fine North Light books are available at your local craft retailer, bookstore or online supplier, or visit our web site at www.mycraftivity.com.